PRAISE FOR JACK FALLA'S PREVIOUS COLLECTION OF ESSAYS, *HOME ICE*

"literary hot chocolate that will warm your heart."
—*The New York Times*

"While *Home Ice* may be a book about hockey and the charm of backyard rinks, it is more than that, too. It is a book about relationships—between fathers and sons, husbands and wives—and how the game can bridge the gaps that commonly occur between generations in a family . . . It's a treasure and one that readers will be happy they searched out. Possibly the best hockey book since Ken Dryden's *The Game*."
—*The Globe and Mail*

"Hockey's foremost writer poses the essential question: 'Have you ever been unhappy skating?' That question could be answered with another question: 'Have you ever been unhappy reading Jack Falla?' Never. If Falla and his fellow rink-makers belong to the 'lunatic fringe,' then count me in. Never has lunacy been so much fun to read about."
—*The Hockey News*

"What a wonderful shock to open a book and for a fantastical moment think that the writer had you in mind when he created it . . . I read *Home Ice* and saw my life come alive on the page . . ."
—*Bostonia Magazine*

". . . a collection of essays that are a mix of the celestial (the poignant family moments) and the terrestrial (the how-to grunt work of actual rink building)."
—*Boston Globe*

"Falla's rink (and this book) enlivens the darkness and cold and pays homage to the New England cultural heritage."
    —*Christian Science Monitor*

"A gentle and powerful book."
    —*Dave Bidini, Author of Tropic of Hockey and The Best Game You Can Name*

PRAISE FOR JACK FALLA'S HOCKEY NOVEL, *SAVED*

"Sportswriter Falla knows a lot about hockey, and this novel is a hilarious look at how players, coaches and owners get through a grueling season in their quest for the trophy. . . . Falla's graphic portrayal of a violent sport (and its colorful players) and his insider's view of how hockey is played, coached and officiated is exciting, surefire entertainment."
    —From the *Publishers Weekly* Starred Review

"Falla covered the NHL for *Sports Illustrated* for many years, and he clearly understands the league, its players, and its idiosyncrasies. He also loves hockey. The flashbacks of kids playing on natural ice during frozen New England winters are heartfelt and genuine. Most novels with a sports backdrop seem forced; seldom do the authors get the 'sports' part right. To borrow a hockey term, Falla records a hat trick: he scores on character, plot, and setting. This reads as realistically as if it were a memoir."
    —From the *Booklist* Review

Open Ice

OPEN ICE

REFLECTIONS AND CONFESSIONS OF A HOCKEY LIFER

JACK FALLA

John Wiley & Sons Canada, Ltd.

Library and Archives Canada Cataloguing in Publication Data

Falla, Jack, 1944-

    Open ice : reflections and confessions of a hockey lifer / Jack Falla.

Includes index.
ISBN 978-0-470-15305-5

    1. Falla, Jack, 1944-. 2. Hockey—Canada. I. Title.
GV847.F34 2008   796.9620971   C2008-902157-6

Production Credits
Cover design: Ian Koo
Interior text design: Mike Chan
Typesetting: Natalia Burobina
Cover images: Stockbyte, Rubberball, Photodisc, Stewart Bell
Printer: Tri-Graphic Printing Ltd.

John Wiley & Sons Canada, Ltd.
6045 Freemont Blvd.
Mississauga, Ontario
L5R 4J3

This book is printed with biodegradable vegetable-based inks on 55lb. recycled cream paper, 100% post-consumer waste.

Printed in Canada

1 2 3 4 5 TRI 12 11 10 09 08

To Barbara

CONTENTS

PREFACE

I was about halfway through writing this book when a friend asked me how *Open Ice* would differ from one of my earlier books, *Home Ice*, that being a collection of essays and memoirs largely centered on my backyard rink and the skating ponds of my youth.

I told him that in writing *Open Ice* I wouldn't be confined by the boards of a rink or the shore of a pond, that in this book I wanted to get out of the backyard and onto a longer, wider road. I wanted to use hockey as a lens through which I look at life, but in this book I would look from the outside in rather than from the inside out. I see *Open Ice* as more of a companion volume to *Home Ice* than a sequel.

Herein I've tried to play the writer's version of "rover"—the player who, in the days of seven-man hockey, had no prescribed position but was free to roam wherever the game, and his instinct for it, prompted him to go. I was often surprised at where I went and what I felt when I got there.

The first of my trips was painful. My spontaneous journey to Rocket Richard's funeral stirred up memories and emotions too long suppressed. That trip also helped me understand (albeit almost a half-century after the fact) how and why hockey became so much a part of my life and work.

Another trip—this to the Chicoutimi, Quebec, grave of the great Montreal goaltender Georges Vezina—proved unsettling, forcing me as it did into an uncomfortable grappling with the looming specter of mortality and with a growing uncertainty in my once strong Roman Catholicism.

But most of the trips were a joy. And none more so than the night I took my then seven-year-old grandson to his first Boston Bruins game and recalled my first game fifty years earlier on a night that changed my life.

I've included accounts of both times my wife, Barbara, and I have skated lock to lock on Ottawa's Rideau Canal, this in the metaphorical shadow of Aurèle Joliat who skated the Rideau when he was in his eighties, something I hope to do in sixteen more winters.

A trip to Ottawa to attend the reunion of the then six living members of the 1956–'60 Montreal Canadiens dynasty that won a record five Stanley Cups in a row turned out to be less about a homage to Henri Richard, Dickie Moore, Jean-Guy

Talbot, Donny Marshall and Tom Johnson—all of whom I saw play many times—and more about Jean Béliveau and the curious way he connected Barbara and me on the first day we met forty years ago.

I've herein tried to explain my fascination with and memories of the old smoke-filled arenas of the National Hockey League's Original Six teams, four of which buildings I covered games in and all of which I saw.

I also went snooping around the Boston area in search of the supposedly extinct rink rat, and was happy and surprised to find that this subspecies of hockey player is still flourishing.

I thought it might be hard to explain why I gave up playing fantasy hockey after winning $800 in two seasons. But a trip to Rome and a Saturday morning in which I sat beneath the priceless art of the Sistine Chapel thinking only of what player I might acquire to replace Los Angeles Kings forward Alexander Frolov convinced me that the synthetic and fraudulent fantasy game was no longer worth the candle.

A trip to a big-box store to buy my first pair of skates in twenty-three years seemed too pedestrian a journey to even think about much less write about. But that trip turned into a year-long odyssey and an inquiry into the intimate bond between skater and skates.

I looked back into the game further and more reverentially than I ever have on the day I went to St. Paul's School in Concord, New Hampshire, to search the school's archives for insight into the life and early death of the fabled and mysterious Hobey Baker and to dip my fingers into the waters of Lower

School Pond, where the greatest American hockey player of his day learned to skate.

A walk from Boston University to Boston Garden to watch the Bruins practice triggered recollections of the days when I cut college classes to catch Bruins practices and of one unforgettable day when I found the Detroit Red Wings taking the ice minus a practice goalie and I asked the Red Wings' Alex Delvecchio if I could play.

I returned to my childhood home in Winchester, Massachusetts, and was surprised to see our old metal garage still standing and bearing the dents of pucks shot into it a half-century ago. The sight got me thinking about my years playing goal and the enduring life lessons I learned.

And in the end I returned to my current home in Natick, Massachusetts, to consider my backyard rink—the Bacon Street Omni—and to grapple with the decision to discontinue it of my own free will or to have the encroachments and humiliations of age force the decision upon me. Do I want to leave or be left?

The writing of a book brings its surprises. In both *Home Ice* and *Open Ice* I was often astonished at the number of people who seemed almost to pop up from my keyboard like the Ghosts of Hockey Past. And I was often surprised by the emotions my memory of those people evoked.

Writing *Open Ice* helped me see what I've long felt: that the game is important to me for reasons that transcend standings, statistics and scores. I remember a day years ago when I had finished giving a guest lecture in a friend's summer term class at Boston University. As we talked briefly in the corridor after my presentation, I told my professor friend that I was headed to Buffalo to attend the NHL Entry Draft. "Why do you go to the draft? They don't play hockey there," he said.

"I go to see my friends," I said, explaining that the NHL is like a tribal gathering. I'd walked a few steps down the corridor and my friend was just closing the door to his classroom when I called back, "Hockey is the only tribe I belong to."

Now, in my mid-sixties and more than fifty years a skater and a fan, I thought it would be a good time to look at the ways in which a game can shape a life. And to do this less by looking back than by looking within.

Jack Falla
Natick, Massachusetts
February 3, 2008

A DEATH IN MONTREAL

Other men are lenses through which we
read our own minds.
—Ralph Waldo Emerson

The last time I saw Maurice Richard he was dead.

It was on Tuesday, May 30, 2000, and I was standing about three feet from his body, which was lying in an open casket on the floor of Le Centre Molson, a hockey arena in Montreal. Looking at him in his white-faced, pale-lipped lifelessness, the meaty hands folded over his stomach, I thought of the first time I'd seen him forty-four years earlier, and about the other death that had brought me to that game.

It was the winter of 1955/'56 when I was eleven years old, and my father had taken me to a Bruins-Canadiens game at Boston Garden. We arrived at our seats—in the first row behind the bright red box seats and thus close to the ice—about twenty minutes before game time. Both teams were on the ice, the players skating nonchalantly through pre-game warm-ups.

"That's Rocket Richard. Numbah 9," my father said in his heavy Boston accent, nudging me and pointing with his rolled-up *Boston Record* to the Montreal player with the thick black, slightly greasy-looking hair swept back along the top and sides of his angular Gallic face. His eyes, so often described as black, were dark green, large and set so deep into their sockets and under such bushy black brows that, thus shaded, they looked like coals. A few dark chest hairs poked over the loosely tied neck of his game shirt. Notwithstanding that he was merely loafing at the blue line, there was, in the dark mien of Maurice Richard, a vague aura of coiled menace. And I wasn't the only one who thought so. Novelist and Nobel laureate William Faulkner, in an essay entitled "An Innocent at Rinkside" in the January 24, 1955, issue of *Sports Illustrated,* described Richard as possessing, "something of the passionate, glittering, fatal, alien quality of snakes."

To the diminishing number of us who saw Richard play, Faulkner's line will forever remain the best physical description of hockey's most passionate, driven and consequential player.

Richard mattered in a way no other hockey players and few other athletes have ever mattered. Wayne Gretzky, Gordie Howe, Mario Lemieux and Bobby Orr were better players and had a larger impact on the record book and box office. But Richard's significance reached beyond the rink and the cash registers. He was a symbol of pride and hope to French Canadians, a people less likely to view themselves as a majority in Quebec than as a minority in English Canada or, worse but not inaccurately during the Rocket's era of the 1940s and '50s, as an oppressed majority in their own province, subjects of an English government, employees of English capitalists and less than *les maîtres chez nous*, masters in their house. In the first half of the last century about 70 percent of the wealth of Quebec was in the hands of English merchants and bankers. And many older French Canadians still refer to the forties and fifties as *La grande noirceur*—the Great Darkness—when to be French in Quebec was to be assigned to a social and economic underclass. To them Richard, the living symbol of what was then French-Canadian hockey dominance, was a light shining in that darkness. He was a man atop the meritocracy of hockey, where skill and resolve prevailed over language, politics and religion. French Canadians saw themselves in Maurice Richard the way some black Americans saw themselves in Jackie Robinson or Muhammed Ali. Richard was hope, and hope—says an old French proverb—is always the last to die.

What happened in the years between the first and last times I saw Richard was a slow comprehension of the man's importance, an understanding that seemed to stir with the long, slow rising of the French blood that pumps through my heart from my mother's side.

My mother died the winter before I saw the Rocket, and those two facts are not as disconnected as they seem.

* * *

My mother's death would have come as a surprise to me had it not been for Mrs. Crotty, one of our Boy Scout leaders. Her revelation came at a scout meeting at her house in January of 1955 when I was playing one of those mid-fifties-era tabletop hockey games, the kind with the metal players painted with NHL uniforms. The Crottys' game came with only two teams, the Montreal Canadiens and the Boston Bruins. I was the Canadiens, and the six players I controlled all had the same black hair and all looked to me as if they had been deliberately designed to bear a slight resemblance to Maurice Richard. I think the Bruins players looked like little metallic Milt Schmidts. I must have been losing that game because during a break—probably when the black marble we used as a puck went flying across the living room—Mrs. Crotty pulled my opponent aside and whispered to him, though not softly enough because I overheard her: "Let him win. His mother is dying."

Mrs. Crotty was a nice lady and I know she meant well. But her dark whispered message told me three things: my mother, who was in the hospital with what I had been told was "a blood disease," was sicker than my family had led me to believe; other people apparently knew this but I was not supposed to know it and, thus, not supposed to talk about it; and if my spinning metal Richards beat the other kid's spinning metal Schmidts, the victory would be meaningless.

I must have made up an excuse about having to get home for supper because I don't recall finishing that game. All I remember is walking home in a state of cold apprehension tempered only by the hope that Mrs. Crotty didn't know what she was talking about. But she did. Four or five weeks later my mother died of what I was told was leukemia. But it was actually ovarian cancer, as I would learn from an aunt—my mother's sister—some forty years later. I don't know why I wasn't told the truth. Maybe I wasn't supposed to know about ovaries, notwithstanding that my mother seems to have had a couple of brass ones. I learned years later that her doctors thought she would die in November during severe hemorrhaging following the birth of a son, Stephen Charles, who lived less than two days. But my mother rallied, came home for Christmas and didn't die until February 9. "She fought like a tiger," my father said. You bet the Over on my mother.

During and after the time of my mother's illness, my father, a fallen-away Bruins fan, started going to games again and often took me with him. I think hockey offered him the balm of distraction for what must have been the metastasizing worry over my mother's sickness and, later, for the deep, unhealable wound of our loss. But it was the reason I got to see Rocket Richard.

My mother was of French descent and my maternal grandmother, who lived with us, though born in Boston, was baptized at St. Paul's Church in Havre Boucher, Nova Scotia, one of the little French villages dotting the northwest shore of that province. Her maiden name was Elizabeth Jeannette King, but her father had been born Jean Roi and anglicized the name to John King only when he moved his family to Boston. It was not uncommon for French Canadians resettling in New England to anglicize their names because, here too, the French were seen as a socially dismissible class of laborers and mill workers stubbornly clinging to their language, their Catholicism and their hockey.

Jean Roi with his wife and children left a farm in Nova Scotia so he could earn more money operating a steam shovel in East Boston. His wife, my great grandmother, resentful about leaving Canada, refused to learn English. Thus, my grandmother, though she grew up in Boston, had to learn French.

My grandmother married a man named Anthony Robertie, whose great-grandfather was a William Robitaille born in Loretteville, Quebec, in 1917. No one in my family knows why Robitaille changed his last name. But my mother was French on both sides.

While I'd been told that my grandmother could speak French, she never spoke it in our house, nor did she speak English with an accent. It surprised me one afternoon when, after my father had remarried and Nana had moved to Manchester, New Hampshire, I heard her speaking French to a man who ran a little variety store in that predominantly Franco-American city. My grandmother was not an overt Francophile, nor was she a hockey fan. She was a quiet, deeply religious woman who walked to daily Mass and who seemed to spend the rest of her time in our kitchen baking bread and biscuits, and putting up grape jelly made from the Concord grapes we grew in our yard and crab apple jelly with fruit from our three apple trees. In the summer she made root beer that to this day is the best beverage I've tasted excepting only fine wines. No matter that she stored the root beer on shelves over the refrigerator where about 10 percent of the bottles exploded with a pop and a hiss, sending sticky brown rivulets running down the white sides of the refrigerator. Nana made all our meals, including the supper of March 18, 1955, about a month after my mother's death, during which Maurice Richard provided me with my first glimpse into my grandmother's French pride.

My father and I were watching the evening news in a small family room off the kitchen when my grandmother walked in. "Look at this, Liz," said my father, gesturing to the grainy news film on the black-and-white television screen where shadowy forms were throwing rocks at what the announcer said was the Montreal Forum and flames licked at what looked like a newsstand. My grandmother asked what was going on and my father explained that National Hockey League president Clarence Campbell had suspended the Montreal Canadiens' and NHL's leading scorer, Maurice Richard, for the last three games of the season and for all of the playoffs for pushing a linesman during a fight in a game in Boston a few nights earlier. The day after Campbell announced the suspension—St. Patrick's Day, which is why I remember these dates—he attended the Montreal-Detroit game at the Forum, where fans pelted him with fruit, eggs and pickled pigs' feet and someone (to this day no one knows if it was a fan or a policeman) set off a tear gas bomb that sent thousands of angry fans pouring onto the streets and gave Detroit the win by forfeit. Having supplied my grandmother with the background of what has since come to be called "the Richard Riot," my late father then did a rude thing. Shifting into a bad imitation of a French-Canadian accent, he said something like, "De Frogs dere, sonofagun, don't like de English guy 'oo suspend Maurice Richard, eh?" (Sometimes you bet the Under on my father.)

In the course of his little gaucherie, my father pronounced Richard's name the way we had always pronounced it and heard it pronounced—Mor-*reece* Ri-*chard*."

"It's Mohr-riss Ri-sharr," my grandmother said, pronouncing the name correctly.

My father laughed at the pronunciation. "Morriss," he said derisively.

"It's Mohr-riss Ri-sharr," Nana said. "I know. I'm French." It was the only time I heard a hardness in my grandmother's voice. The only time I saw her stand up to my father.

I would go on mispronouncing Richard's name for another forty-five years until my daughter Tracey married a man named Maurice Henri whose father and grandfather—both named Maurice Henri—speak French. It was only when I heard the name repeatedly and correctly pronounced, that I started saying it the way my grandmother said it, Mohr-riss.

* * *

I inherited Nana's love of cooking (though none of her skill), which explains why I was at the stove in my daughter's house making shrimp and andouille sausage jambalaya for a party on the evening of Saturday, May 27, 2000. Hunched over our old black gas stove, Nana was like Lionel Hampton leaning over his vibraphone—all deft moves, relaxed confidence and superb results. Me? I'm more like a freshman glockenspieler in the high school band—scared but willing. That evening, as I shuffled and flipped the contents of two sauté pans—the gratuitously ostentatious flipping being solely for the entertainment of my grandson Demetre, who clapped and went into paroxyms of gleeful kicking if a shrimp flew out of the pan—Barbara called to me from the living room.

"Jack, come here. Quick," she said.

"Can't. I'm in full flight out here," I said.

"Rocket Richard died," she said.

I turned the burners to low, scooped up my grandson and hurried to the living room. There, on television, ESPN hockey analyst Barry Melrose was talking of Richard's death from abdominal cancer at 5:40 that afternoon at Hôtel Dieu, Montreal's oldest hospital. Melrose struggled to explain Richard's iconic importance to the people of French Canada, but nothing did that better than his news that the Quebec government would give Richard a state funeral such as would normally be accorded only a handful of the highest-ranking political leaders or national heroes. There was also an announcement that, on Tuesday, Richard's body would lie in state at the Molson Centre, the 21,273-seat arena that in 1996 replaced the legendary Montreal Forum as the home of *Le Club de Hockey Canadien*.

"I've got to go to that," I told Barbara, who reminded me that I also had to be at a friend's wedding in South Dakota that Friday. My original plan had been to leave Sunday and to drive to South Dakota, solitary long-distance driving being high on my list of life's minor pleasures. "I'll fly out on Thursday," I said. Barbara, to her eternal credit, never said a word about a round-trip short-notice coach ticket from Boston to Rapid City, South Dakota, costing about $1,500. Maybe she was too surprised that

I would go to a funeral of any kind much less to a celebrity funeral. I'd never done anything like this.

I didn't even go to my mother's funeral, although that was not my decision. I think my father and other relatives believed that it would be too heart-wrenching for my eight-year-old sister and me to be in the same room as our mother's dead body and that our presence would have been difficult for the other mourners. In hindsight it was not a good decision. Sometimes you have to see the body to let go of the person and accept the finality of death. But, in that chaotic time, the decision seemed among the least of my sadnesses, since I then, and for a long time afterward, viewed wakes and funerals as merely symbolic and ritualistic as opposed to death itself, which is so chillingly final. Going to the funeral wasn't going to bring my mother back. I did not cry on the day of my mother's death or even in the days immediately afterward. I've always attributed this to shock or to a kind of emotional bracing I was able to do following the unpleasantness at Mrs. Crotty's house. I think it would have been different, and in the long run helpfully so, had I gone to my mother's funeral.

Today I go to the wakes and funerals of friends and relatives and try to say the correct things. I feel an honest compassion for people's loss. But I have to force myself to go and, at wakes, I rarely stay long. Before Richard's death, I had never been to a celebrity funeral, nor had I ever thought of going to one. I generally disdain the celebrity culture, don't ask for autographs, don't have a current sports hero and can name very few movie stars. When Wayne Gretzky gave me a hockey stick after

I'd written a profile of him, I used the stick in a pond hockey game, then on my backyard rink and finally in a street hockey game where someone stepped on the blade and the stick was relegated to a few years' use as a tomato stake before I threw it away. My childhood sports hero was the late Jacques Plante, a goalie and teammate of Maurice Richard's in the Canadiens dynasty that won a record five consecutive Stanley Cups from 1956 to 1960. Plante died in Switzerland in 1986 but, even if he had died in Montreal, a six-hour drive from my home in Natick, Massachusetts, I would not have gone to the funeral. The sudden and costly decision to go to Richard's wake and funeral is the single most out-of-character act of my life.

I'm a writer, but I had no assignment to cover the funeral; nor did I make the phone calls that probably would have gotten me an assignment. I had no media pass or special access. I had to scramble for a hotel room. I made the trip alone and at my own expense, not truly knowing why I was going or what to expect.

As I drove northwest on I-89 through the Green Mountains of Vermont toward the Quebec border, I thought of Richard and what he had meant to the people of Quebec, to hockey and to me. Three years earlier, on the occasion of the fiftieth anniversary of *The Hockey News*, I'd been assigned to write five essays, one on each decade of the *News*'s existence from 1947 to 1997. To research the first of these essays it was necessary to delve into Richard's life and career. I thought I knew my hockey history and of course I knew Richard was the first player to score fifty goals in fifty games, which he did in 1944/'45, something only four other players (Mike Bossy, Wayne Gretzky, Mario Lemieux and Brett Hull) have done. But it was his iron resolve and importance to French Canadians that surprised me.

* * *

Joseph Henri Maurice Richard was born on August 4, 1921, in Bordeaux, Quebec. He was the eldest of the eight children of railroad worker Onésime and Alice Laramée Richard. He began skating at age four and would later say of his childhood, "Many days I had my skates on while I ate supper. Then I would go out and play more."

He often skated alone until ten o'clock at night along the shoreline of Rivière des Prairies, a river so treacherous that local authorities often closed it to skaters. But Richard was no mere skater. He was a boy possessed. When he played his way into the Canadiens 1942 tryout camp, coach Dick Irvin kept him on the roster, not because of his skills but because, as Irvin said, "I never in my life saw a rookie with such a desire to make good."

Said Canadiens left-winger Hector "Toe" Blake, "Richard lives to score goals."

Following Richard's 1942/'43 rookie season, Irvin put him on Montreal's first line with Blake and center Elmer Lach. "The Punch Line," as it came to be called, led *Les Canadiens* to their first Stanley Cup in thirteen years. Richard erased playoff records with twelve goals in nine games. In a semifinal game against Toronto, the player that teammate Ray Getliffe had now nicknamed "Rocket" for his explosive speed from the blue line to the goal, scored all of Montreal's goals in a 5–1 win.

But Richard did not merely score goals in big numbers. He scored with an élan that fired the imagination of the crowds jamming the Forum to see him. "There are goals and there are Richard goals," said Irvin. "Richard goals have flair."

"He's on fire all the time he's on the ice," said Montreal general manager Frank Selke.

So completely did Richard capture the hearts of Canadiens fans that legendary sportswriter Herbert Warren Wind—who would later write for *The New Yorker* but was, in the mid-fifties, a writer for *Sports Illustrated*—described the Montreal crowd's reaction to a Richard goal by observing that the fans "would roar like one huge happy lion, the most jubilant hullabaloo you can hear in the sports world. It is not an extravagant tribute." Wind went on to write that Richard's "hold on the public has no parallel in sport . . . unless it be the country-wide adoration that the people of Spain have from time to time heaped on the rare master matador."

It was against my Boston Bruins that Richard scored the most matadorial of his 544 goals, the one best typifying his intensity and fire. On April 8, 1952, in the first period of the seventh game of a semifinal series in Montreal, Richard was knocked unconscious and cut over the left eye when his head collided with an opponent's knee. A doctor stitched the cut, but Richard, obviously concussed, spent most of the rest of the game on the trainer's table. When he returned to the Canadiens bench late in the third period, he had to ask Elmer Lach the score and the time remaining because Richard couldn't focus his eyes on the clock. The game was tied 1–1 with three and a half minutes left when Richard hopped over the boards on a line change and took a pass from Butch Bouchard at center ice. Accounts of that goal say Richard outskated the backchecking Murray Henderson and Real Chevrefils, then one of the best skaters in the league, carried the puck wide around defenseman Bob Armstrong and outskated defenseman Bill Quackenbush to the right corner, where Richard hit the brakes, cut sharply in front of the Boston net and sent an ankle-high shot past Bruins goalie Sugar Jim Henry to win the game and the series. "What a terrifying sight for a goalie," Henry later told the Montreal *Gazette*, "There was nothing like the Rocket at full speed."

Said Richard: "My head was all foggy. I had a hazy idea of what I was supposed to do. And I did it."

Once, walking through the Boston Garden with my father, I glanced into the open door of the building's private dining room, the Madison Square Garden Club, and saw a copy of the now famous photograph taken minutes after that goal. It showed Richard standing erect, with blood flowing down his cheek and neck from the bandage above his left eye, and Jim Henry, bowing slightly, his right eye blackened and nose broken from a high stick in a previous game, shaking hands at center ice. But moments later in the Canadiens dressing room Richard began sobbing uncontrollably, then went into convulsions and had to be sedated. "That beautiful bastard," said *Montreal Herald* sportswriter Elmer Ferguson, "he scored semi-conscious."

* * *

Even as an adolescent I knew from reading newspapers and sports magazines that Richard was more than a seething and driven scoring machine. He was the fleur-de-lis made flesh, a human flag for the simmering resentments of French Canadians, whose admiration of the man was made angrily manifest in that riot I had seen on television.

Such was the feeling among French Canadians for Richard that a story on the Richard Riot in *Maclean's*, the Canadian news magazine, reported that a French-speaking typesetter in the Montreal *Gazette*'s composing room broke down and cried as he set type for the story announcing Richard's suspension. And that one of the many angry letters to Clarence Campbell said, "If Richard's name was Richardson you would have a different verdict." For weeks after Campbell's decision, Quebec housewives boycotted Campbell's soups, notwithstanding that there was no connection between the food company and the NHL president.

What neither I nor anyone else knew at that time was that the Richard Riot was striking the first sparks of Quebec's so-called Quiet Revolution, a political and social movement that would openly divide Quebec into the now famous "two solitudes"—French and English—and culminate in the still-raging arguments over Quebec sovereignty. For many French Canadians, the flames from the burning of Auguste Belanger's newsstand on the night of March 17, 1955, cast the first light into *La grande noirceur.*

To Richard the night was "terrible . . . awful . . . people might have been killed," he reportedly told a friend. The next day Richard went on radio and, speaking in French and English, asked the people of Montreal to accept Campbell's verdict. "So that no further harm will be done, I would like to ask everyone to get behind the team," said Richard, "and to help the boys win from the Rangers and Detroit. I will come back next year to help the club and the younger players win the Cup." It was a remarkable gesture for a man who was repeatedly a target of ethnic slurs.

"Dirty French bastard" and "French pea soup" were among the insults opposing players yelled at Richard, according to a *Maclean's* interview with Inspector William Minogue, the officer in charge of security during Canadiens games and thus a person often within earshot of the rink. (Anyone who would use "pea soup" as a pejorative clearly had never tasted my grandmother's ham-hocks-and-onion split-pea soup.) Richard occasionally retaliated on the ice, but he never let himself be politicized. "I'm a hockey player, just a hockey player," he'd say when asked to comment on a political issue. "Hockey and politics don't mix" was also a line he routinely grabbed out of his inventory, but it is not as revealing as another of his responses: "hockey is my métier." Yet what he said didn't matter. Maurice Richard was the standard-bearer for Quebec nationalism.

* * *

It was early afternoon when I pulled into Montreal and checked into Le Manoir Le Moyne, an apartment-style hotel about a block

from the old Montreal Forum and within walking distance of
Le Centre Molson (since re-named Le Centre Bell). Because
the hotel is so close to the Forum it was, in the 1980s, a popular
place for visiting teams to stay. I'd stayed there many a night
while covering the Canadiens, so it was more out of habit than
forethought that I came out of the hotel onto De Maisonneuve
and, instead of turning right toward the Molson Centre, turned
left toward the old Forum. I shouldn't have bothered. The Forum
was a mess, shrouded by metal staging and surrounded by
those ramshackle graffiti-marred plywood walls used to screen
construction sites. What was once the "Cathedral of Hockey" was
in the process of being turned into a Cineplex, which to me is
like turning the Louvre into a video arcade. Only the huge cranes,
the hydraulic excavators and one of the office trailers carried a
hint of the building's storied past. Small, neat lettering on much
of the equipment indicated it was owned by the Moore Leasing
Co. I had read somewhere that the Moore whose name adorned
the trailer was multimillionaire Richard "Dickie" Moore, Rocket
Richard's linemate for most of the 1950s and the man Richard
said was the best left wing he'd ever skated with. The paint job
on the office trailer was in the Moore corporate colors, which
are also the Canadiens' team colors—*bleu, blanc, rouge.*

As I completed my walk around the Forum and headed east
on St. Catherine Street,* I thought about the way the Forum had
always impressed and intimidated me.

I'd been in the building dozens of times, even skated there
once in a media game, but on every occasion I felt like a high

---

* Montreal's street signs are now all French, so that has become "rue Ste-Catherine."
However, local English speakers know most of the main arteries by English names, as
reflected in this book.

school kid who'd taken Catherine Deneuve to the junior prom—
self-consciously respectful, dangerously out of my depth. But
I was never more distracted than when I was in the Canadiens'
dressing room, the *sanctum sanctorum* not only of the building but of the hockey world. I went there ostensibly to conduct
post-game player interviews, but I always spent a few moments
gawking like a tourist at the small drawings of Canadiens Hall-
of-Famers lining the walls and at the words of Canadian poet
John McCrae written in 1915 and printed, in French and English, beneath the pictures: *"Nos bras meurtris vous tendent le
flambeau, à vous toujours de le porter bien haut!* To you from
failing hands we throw the torch, be yours to hold it high." In the
eyes of French Canadians, no one held that torch higher than
Maurice Richard or, with it, cast a wider light. At the closing
ceremonies for the building, the Canadiens introduced many
of the great players from the team's past. One by one Jean Béliveau, Guy Lafleur, Serge Savard and others stepped onto the
Forum ice for the final time amid huge cheers from a capacity
crowd. But when the public address announcer introduced the
final player—Maurice Richard—the cheering would not stop.
Every time the volume seemed to be falling, it would pick up
again like a succession of waves surging up a beach; for almost
ten minutes a standing-room crowd—French and English—
gave Richard one of the greatest and most prolonged ovations
in sports history: everyone pouring out their admiration, the
French pouring out their gratitude.

I walked east on St. Catherine to De la Montagne, then
across Boulevard René Lévesque (it used to be Dorchester but

was re-named for the late Quebec separatist leader) toward De la Gauchetière and the four-year-old Centre Molson. I'd never been in that building, but I had no trouble recognizing it because there on the north wall was a several-stories-high photo of Maurice Richard—his head up and those huge dark eyes fairly exploding out of his face as he pushed onto his right skate out of that wide-track stance that had made him so hard for defensemen to knock down. Indeed, the newspapers that day and the next had carried stories of Richard's "Siebert goal," a reference to Detroit's 225-pound veteran defenseman Earl "Babe" Siebert, who, in a desperate effort to stop a Richard rush in a game in Montreal, threw himself across the Rocket's back at the Detroit blue line only to have the 180-pound Richard carry Siebert and the puck all the way to the Detroit goalmouth, where the Rocket cut right to left across the crease before flipping the puck high into the Detroit net. Said an awed Siebert: "Any guy who can carry me 60 feet and put the puck in the net, more power to him."

As I approached the arena I saw the line of mourners shuffling along the sidewalk beneath the huge photo and the sign reading *Maurice Richard—Le Rocket*. The line moved at a slow, shuffling pace and I calculated that it would take me ten minutes or so to reach the arena floor. That was important to me because I have an almost agoraphobic dislike of lines and crowds and go to enormous lengths to avoid them. I routinely attend the uncrowded mid-afternoon screenings of movies, grocery-shop as soon as the stores open, get to airports two to three hours before departure and never go near a bank, post office or dry cleaner on a Saturday. But on this day I simply took my place in line and was curiously undismayed even when I got to the arena entrance and realized the line snaked down a long concourse, then down a flight of stairs through the stadium's lower bowl and finally into one of those switchback mazes of velvet ropes such as one sees at airline counters and amusement parks. The last time I'd stood in a line like this was seventeen years earlier, at Disney World's Pirates of the Caribbean, with children all around me chanting, "Yo ho, yo ho, the pirate's life for me." At least this time I got to listen to *Ave Maria.*

There was little talk in the arena line, just a kind of low murmur, and most of what I heard was in French with only a smattering of English. A man in a No. 9 Canadiens' white game shirt held the hand of a little boy, apparently the man's son, dressed in a No. 9 red Canadiens' game shirt. There was a man in a wheelchair and several babies in strollers; none of the babies was crying. Women made up at least a third of the mourners and nearly all of the women I heard spoke French. When I heard an English voice, it was usually a man's. I think most of the men were sports fans, but many of the women came for other reasons.

As I entered the arena at the top of the stairs, the *Ave Maria* was being sung softly over the sound system, and the song immediately took me back to my childhood in a Catholic grammar school in Massachusetts and my years as an altar boy. These days I'm what a friend calls "a submarine Catholic—you surface only in times of trouble." True enough, I suppose, but if Catholicism is lately less my path to spirituality it has always been part of my culture and I was deeply moved and curiously saddened by hearing again the Latin I had heard so many times as a boy:

Ave Maria
gratia plena
Dominus tecum...

There was no ice in the arena, all advertising was draped in black and four small spotlights in the dark ceiling drew your eyes to the body of Maurice Richard, which was where it belonged: under the red, white and blue banner commemorating his retired No. 9 and between the faceoff circles in the area hockey players call "the slot." It's where goal scorers work. There were two photos near the casket, one of Richard skating, and another of the aging Richard wearing his red game shirt and holding a torch.

As the line approached the casket, two ushers—a man and a woman—directed half of us to the right and half to the left. They worked wordlessly, gesturing occasionally with their hands as to the direction they wanted you to go. I went to the left past a woman usher in a dark blazer and skirt. As I'd seen for fifteen years at the old Forum—where the women ushers wore red blazers, dark skirts and low heels—Canadiens ushers are neither fashionable nor unfashionable. They are simply correct.

Thank God his eyes are closed, was my first thought as I drew close to the embalmed body of Maurice Richard. I wouldn't have wanted to look into those eyes and see that the fire was out. I was struck by the size of his stomach until I remembered that it was weight—he gained about a pound a season—that finally stopped him on that September day in 1960 when, after scoring four goals on Jacques Plante in practice, the Rocket announced his retirement. Now, standing beside his casket, I did not know what to do and so I prayed. I said a Hail Mary and made the sign of the cross as I walked by. Some people bowed their heads, many wept, some touched the casket, and a few reached out and touched the corpse itself. I did not think of doing that. What business have I touching Maurice Richard.

I'd read that the Quebec government had offered to drape the casket in the blue-and-white fleur-de-lis of Quebec. But the family, now led by Maurice Richard Jr., eldest son of Maurice and the late Lucille Richard's seven children, politely refused because they wanted a simple religious ceremony and did not want to politicize the services. Or, as jingoistic English-Canadian TV hockey commentator Don Cherry was to say, "People in Quebec loved the Rocket, but he was our hero too." On this day, Canada's French and English were on the same sad page.

Not once in the half-hour or so I was in the arena did I see a mourner stop long enough to hold up the line. Everyone moved at the same respectful funereal pace. I have never seen such civility in a crowd.

As I took my last look at Richard and walked toward the lower concourse, I noticed a small gathering of people in an area about twenty feet behind the casket. They were apparently family members, but the only one I recognized was the five-foot-seven, silver-haired, impossibly distinguished-looking Henri "Pocket Rocket" Richard, the Rocket's younger brother by fifteen years and, for the first five of Henri's twenty NHL seasons, Maurice's center. Henri once said that, because of the age gap, he and Maurice didn't talk much and—in what surely was an exaggeration—that all the conversations they had about hockey would not fill one sixty-minute audio tape. But in the next day's Montreal *Gazette*, Henri recalled his first NHL game and what Maurice told him before he took to the ice: "I was very nervous but he just said something to me about picking up the torch. And once we started playing I felt good."

Henri did more than just pick up the fabled torch. He carried it to a record eleven Stanley Cups (among North American pro athletes only ex-Boston Celtic Bill Russell has eleven championships), but while he was popular with fans—and a better skater, stickhandler, checker and playmaker than Maurice—he never touched the hearts of Montrealers the way his brother did.

Henri was shaking hands and talking to people as if he were standing in a small neighborhood funeral parlor. I thought of going over but it seemed intrusive, so I walked with the crowd toward the exit, passing a condolence book in which a mourner had written: "My first words were Mama, Papa and Maurice Richard." I could not think of anything to write. The next day I read that a new condolence book was needed about every three hours until the building closed at 11 P.M., by which time 115,000 mourners had filed past Richard's body.

Heading for the exit, I walked past two women who looked to be in their sixties, one of them softly singing the *Ave Maria* in French: "*Ave Maria!/ Je vous salue, Marie, pleine de grace.*" she sang as if to herself.

Many of us were misty-eyed as we walked out into the late-afternoon sun. And why not. It was, after all, a wake. *C'est normal,* I thought, and blinked away my tears and that day thought no more about them.

Back at the hotel I heard reports that mourners were already queuing up for the thousand seats the Richard family had set aside for the general public in the three-thousand-seat Cathédral Notre Dame. The rest of the pews for the 10 A.M. Requiem High Mass were reserved for dignitaries that would include Canadian Prime Minister Jean Chrétien, former prime minister Brian Mulroney and Quebec Premier Lucien Bouchard. A huge and temporary television screen in Place d'Armes would make it possible for about seven thousand mourners who could not get seats to watch a telecast of the service. I would not be among them. I didn't have time.

The next morning I was in full get-away mode—preoccupied with checkout time, with plotting escape routes from a city in which many streets would be shut down for the cortège and funeral, and with worrying about getting home in time to prepare for my South Dakota trip. I was also looking for a drugstore so I could buy a box of tissues because of a cold I'd caught the previous day. I bought the tissues, then hustled up to the corner of St. Catherine and Stanley Streets and stood on the sidewalk east of the Banque de Montréal that had on it a sign reading: *Nos Hommages Monsieur Richard.* From here I could watch the funeral procession before I had to get my car out of the garage and hightail it home. But despite my summer cold and logistical distractions, I was surprised to find myself just a little weepy, as I had been the day before. It didn't seem so normal this time.

Helicopters followed the cortège from Le Centre Molson north on Montagne Street then east onto St. Catherine, a street that had seen so many Canadiens Stanley Cup parades that the team PR department once issued a media advisory saying: "Tomorrow's Stanley Cup parade will follow the usual route." Two blocks to my right, fourteen black limousines made the turn onto St. Catherine, and slowly the applause grew and swept down the queues lining the sidewalks. It was polite applause. Restrained. And with no voices. There was a way to comport oneself this morning and the people of Montreal knew it. A woman stepped onto the street and placed a red rose on the black hood of the hearse carrying Maurice Richard's body. The hearse rolled slowly past a shop window that had in it a single gray seat from the old Forum—seat No. 5 but with no row or section number—and a bouquet of daisies on it and a hand-lettered sign: *Merci #9*. And down the street went the black cars, with people coming off the sidewalks to walk behind the procession past Banque Nationale, Crabtree & Evelyn, Le Steakhouse and Le Sex Shoppe, east to St. Denis Street, then south to Notre Dame Boulevard and west to the cathedral.

But I was in a hurry. I hustled back to the hotel to watch a few minutes of the service on television. I was packing my suitcase as the TV showed the pallbearers walking with the casket down the center aisle. They were all former teammates, French and English, the flower of a club its French-Canadian fans call *Nos glorieux*. There was Jean Béliveau, who is to Richard as Joe DiMaggio is to Babe Ruth; Elmer Lach; Butch Bouchard; Ken Mosdell; Dickie Moore; Ken Reardon; Gerry McNeil; and, on the front left corner with his right hand on the casket, Henri Richard, who was crying.

I listened to the rest of the service on English CBC Radio in the car as I picked my way out of the city and over the St. Lawrence River via the Champlain Bridge.

On the radio Jean-Claude Cardinal Turcotte, archbishop of Montreal, delivered a homily that ended with a mention of Richard's love of fishing, and whimsically speculated how the fishermen among Jesus' apostles might greet Monsieur Richard. "I can clearly see Maurice going to meet them. They'll have a lot to say"; and then, after a pause, Cardinal Turcotte added, "Happy fishing, Maurice." Mohr-riss he pronounced it. There was a childish simplicity, almost a naivety to the story. It touched me. I then heard in the background a sound I'd never heard before—three thousand people and one cardinal archbishop applauding in a church.

Afterward a composed Maurice Richard Jr. began a brief eulogy that he delivered in a soft calm voice, but I don't remember much of what he said because I was by now neither calm nor composed. "Emotions leak," my wife Barbara, a social worker, has long told me. But that morning the entombed emotions of forty-five years, raised by the events and connections of the past two days, exploded like a bottle of my grandmother's root beer, unleashing a lachrymal flood of tears and mucus. I heard myself fighting for breath and knew I hadn't cried like this more than two or three times in my life. It was as if Maurice Richard's death and the accompanying outpouring of a people's love, my immersion in the French-Canadian culture, my thoughts of my mother and grandmother and of my childhood and of the distant pull of my family's Catholicism had raised feelings I'd long ago buried. Or thought I had. And so I cried less for Maurice Richard and his family and the French-Canadian people than for my own losses—for a mother loved but incompletely grieved, for a grandmother loved but inadequately thanked, for a sense of my own Frenchness—the dominant half of what I am—nearly lost in the dark aftermath of death. For my own *grande noirceur.* The tears were long overdue and much interest had accumulated. I was glad I'd put the box of tissues in the passenger seat. I should have pulled off the road but I kept driving.

The immediate result of this crying and driving is that I bogeyed Vermont. I hurtled past my exit without even a nod of recognition, not realizing I was off course until I saw a sign directing me to the USA via Newport, Vermont, and I-91, which is in the northeast corner of the state. I'd intended to drive home by picking up I-89 at Swanton in the northwest corner. A backup of cars at Customs and Immigration gave me time to compose myself and clean my driving glasses. I used my right thumbnail to scrape the now calcified salt stains off my lenses.

The Montreal radio station's signal had faded by the time I cleared Customs and headed south on I-91, which swings east into New Hampshire and White Mountain National Forest. Far to the east rose the majestic Presidential Range, including

5,363-foot Mount Madison, which forty-three years earlier I had climbed with Mrs. Crotty's son Edmund and others from my Boy Scout troop.

SHORT SHIFTING IN FANTASY LAND

The victor is by victory undone.
—John Dryden

I hit bottom in the Sistine Chapel at the Vatican in Rome on the morning of Saturday, March 17, 2007. Barbara and I were nearing the end of a ten-day Italian vacation. I was maxed out on cherubs and Madonnas, tired from traipsing around Naples, Florence, Capri and Rome, and a bit worse off for the bottle of Tuscan wine I'd enjoyed at dinner and was enjoying a lot less on this morning.

We'd been in the chapel for about ten minutes when I headed for one of the marble benches that run the length of both walls. I sat slumped over, staring at the floor, looking and feeling like a hockey player who'd just finished a tough shift, which, in a manner of speaking, I had. Barb sat beside me. "Cowboy up," she said, loading yet another film into her camera. (Whether taking photographs on vacation or playing hockey on the back-yard rink, Barb takes the Alexander Ovechkin approach to shooting: blast away often enough and you're bound to come up with something.)

Sitting amid the multilingual murmur of tourists and tour guides and beneath what might be the highest concentration of priceless art in the world, I was thinking not of the genius of Michelangelo, who had created the art, or of Pope Julius II, who had paid for it (albeit slowly), or even of the eternal life it represented. I was thinking about Alexander Frolov and how the then slumping Los Angeles Kings forward was killing me and how when I got home on Monday—the weekly trade deadline in my fantasy hockey league—I would trade his Kremlin butt back to Moscow or Carjackistan or wherever he came from.

The streaky Frolov was a third-line forward on my entry in the 2,032-team Fantasy Hockey Pool operated by CDM Sports of St. Louis, Missouri, and, judging from the names of some of the teams (Hab A Chance, Let's Go Flames, Top Corner), made up of people who spend too much time poring over hockey stat sheets on their laptops on the back tables at Tim Hortons or Dunkin' Donuts. I'd picked my team while sitting in Italo DeMasi's barber chair in Natick, Massachusetts, and entered the team under my own name on the off chance that I might break into the top 100, whose team names get published daily on the fantasy league's web site. I debuted in the top 100 at No. 54 on December 15, 2006. I would go on to win $500 for having the No. 1 team in December. I was No. 6 on January 6 (a morning after Frolov had scored two goals), knocked around in the teens for most of the season and finished the season at No. 29, good for another $100.

On the day we'd left for Italy I was No. 20 and much under the illusion that I could win the pool, thus my obsession with replacing the suddenly unproductive Frolov. I was idly wondering who I could put in Frolov's slot (Doug Weight? Darcy Tucker?) when I saw Barb raise her camera toward the chapel's ceiling. Tourists aren't allowed to take photos inside the chapel, but Barb was using her medium-length lens as a telescope to more closely examine the art. I slowly looked up, tracking the general direction of her camera. That's when I saw God.

God was reaching out his right hand to touch the hand of Adam in the famous Michelangelo fresco *The Creation of Adam,* located at the mid-point of the Sistine Chapel's ceiling. I had known that the work was somewhere in the chapel but I'd always thought it had its own room. Or dome. I didn't know it was among the forty-nine paintings on the main ceiling. But there it was between *The Separation of Sky and Water* (good move seeing as how that was the first step toward making ice) and *The Creation of Eve* (a great move for obvious reasons). I was Godsmacked. I forgot Alexander Frolov and wondered for a moment about the divine spark that may have passed between the hands of God and Adam. I thought that of all the art and beauty I'd seen in Italy it was this painting that would live in my mind forever.

And then I went back to thinking about Alexander Frolov. But that wasn't my mistake. My mistake was *talking* about Alexander Frolov.

"I think I'm going to drop Frolov," I said to Barb as our tour group shuffled out of the chapel and toward St. Peter's Basilica.

"You're using up your minutes," Barb said. The reference was to the two-minute rule we'd established (OK, Barb established) in the 2005/'06 NHL season, the second season in which I'd played fantasy hockey. The deal was that I got two minutes a day to boast, bitch, analyze or otherwise bore her with talk of my fantasy team. Unused minutes did not accumulate and could not be carried over to future days or even redeemed for magazine subscriptions. It was use them or lose them. Indeed, one of the first things I learned about fantasy hockey, and fantasy sports in general, is that most women do not want to hear about, much less talk about, a guy's fantasy hockey team. I learned this the way I've learned most things about women: the hard way.

It was during the 2004 play-offs that Barbara and I were having dinner with two women sportswriters at a French-Cambodian restaurant in Boston. One of the women had been a student of mine at Boston University and was now a national hockey writer in town to cover the Boston/Montreal series. Her friend was an editor and sometime writer in the sports department of a New Jersey daily. We were about halfway through the meal when someone mentioned the name of Boston winger Glen Murray. "He's on my fantasy team," I said. Big mistake. All three women looked aghast, the writers expressing their dismay that I, too, played fantasy hockey and offering Barbara their sympathies for what they thought, rightly, at the time, were the filibusters she had to listen to as I explained my team's shifting fortunes and the various roster moves I had made or was contemplating. The women were clearly disappointed in me. Disillusioned. But no one could tell me exactly why except to say that guys who played fantasy sports spent too much time talking about them and that the entire concept of "managing" a team that you didn't own and didn't have any real control over was, somehow, immature and self-delusional. I was saved by the dessert cart.

The first time I played any fantasy sport I was in something called *The Hockey News* Supreme Pool. I did well. I still remember the night late in that season when I was reading *The Hockey News* and first found my name among the top 100 teams in the pool. That was Tampa Bay right-winger Martin St. Louis's breakout year. I'd seen St. Louis play at the University of Vermont, thought he was hugely underrated and misused in his early NHL years, and was happy to draft him onto my team and happier beyond all telling to watch him win the Hart Trophy as the league's most valuable player, lead the Bolts to the Stanley Cup and bring my fantasy team to a top-75 finish for which I made roughly three times my entry fee. When the check arrived that summer (sports fantasy leagues pay off almost as slowly as Pope Julius II), I photocopied the accompanying letter of congratulations, left a copy on Barb's pillow and mailed a copy to the two lady sportswriters who'd beaten up on me in the restaurant. I am a graceless winner. But not a misogynist. I split my winnings with my granddaughter Ella, the only female in my family who had not made fun of me for what had quickly become my obsession with fantasy hockey. Ella was two years old at the time and had not yet learned to speak. But she was a good listener and seemed not to mind when I carried her around the house while talking endlessly of Grandpa Jack's shrewd manipulations of his fantasy roster. Indeed, she often fell asleep.

"Why don't women like guys who play fantasy sports?" I asked my writer friend and neighbor, Michelle Seaton, who contributes occasional sports features to *Only a Game,* a nationally syndicated show aired on National Public Radio. Ms. Seaton's emailed reply, in its embarrassing entirety, reads:

> I think it's the word fantasy. That word leads to ideas of sex. And porn and all those other nasty things women say "Yuck" to. No. That's not quite it. But it IS the word fantasy. There's something about it. It can't be associated with something that is really a hobby. [It's] something that takes hours and hours of thought and effort but isn't actually real.
>
> I think of that fantasy stuff as Dungeons and Dragons but with sports. And when I think of that, I think of pudgy guys who like to hang out in finished basements. [Guys] who still wear baseball caps backward and who have never kissed a girl. I know that's not you, but that is the stereotype in my head.

"How does she know it's not you?" Barb said when I showed her the email.

Why don't women like men who play fantasy sports, I asked Debra Waldeyer, a copy editor in the sports department of *The Record,* Hackensack, New Jersey. She said it was a loyalty issue, that a fan should cheer for a real team and be true to that team. "Fantasy sports players can never wear body paint, too many colors for too little skin," she said.

I suspect that my daughter Tracey may have come nearest the truth about women and fantasy sports when she told me: "When you guys play fantasy sports you talk to each other and when you're talking to each other you're not talking to us."

I wasn't listening to them either. I kept playing. I finished out of the money in 2005/'06, the season following the NHL lockout, because I over-weighted on guys who hadn't played much during the 2004/'05 shutdown (talking about you, Jarome Iginla). That was the year I drove Barb to institute the two-minute rule. Losers talk more than winners.

The 2006/'07 season was my best ever. I was in the top 40 for most of the season and, for a time in January, threatening to sneak into first place. But it was my worst season, too, and this for a reason I never expected.

I jumped from No. 9 to No. 8 on January 29, 2007, a Monday night on which Patrice Bergeron, the only Boston Bruin on my team, scored a goal in a 6–1 Bruins loss to the New York Rangers. I felt good about the goal and the five points it gave me. I would have preferred to see the Bruins win but, mainly, I was happy with my points and my bump in the standings and didn't much care about the Bruins loss.

My view got even narrower on February 26 when the Bruins, my favorite team for fifty years and my family's favorite for five generations, played Atlanta, whose goalie, Kari Lehtonen, was on my team. I had a 4:15 A.M. wake-up call so I went to bed after the second period with the score tied 2–2. The first thing I did when I awoke was to snap on my computer, log onto NHL.com and check the previous night's scores. The first score posted was Atlanta 3 – Boston 2. My right fist shot into the air and I whispered a hoarse, "Yessssss." Lehtonen had netted me five points for the goalie win. It was the first time in my life I'd cheered a Bruins loss.

But why not cheer their loss and my gain? Professional teams in every sport are made up of mercenaries. Why shouldn't I value an Atlanta win, which could help net me a few dollars, over a Bruins win that would have netted me nothing because Bergeron had neither scored nor assisted. I was only doing what anyone in my position would do, rooting for myself.

Ten days later I looked at the TV listings and saw that the Bruins were hosting Colorado in a locally televised game. But by this time I had dropped the slumping Bergeron and had no player on either roster. I saw that there was another televised game on the Versus cable network. But I did not have a player in that game either. So I didn't watch hockey. I watched a two-hour segment of Ken Burns' *Jazz*, a film I'd already seen three times, on a video cassette I'd taken out of the library. Then I went to bed. I didn't even check scores.

As the NHL regular season entered its final weeks, my fantasy team bounced from No. 12 on March 19 to a low of No. 46 on March 31, by which point I had almost stopped watching hockey entirely except for an occasional Bruins Saturday matinee or a nationally televised game involving Pittsburgh's Sidney Crosby, who was on my fantasy team but was someone I'd watch even if he wasn't. I was enjoying fantasy hockey. I was not enjoying ice hockey. I could have been, should have been, enjoying *both*. That's how it was in the beginning. Fantasy hockey at first enhanced my knowledge of the NHL and broadened the scope of my interest. I pored over box scores. Looked forward to particular games involving "my" players and, in general, enjoyed hockey more than I had at any time since the 1980s when I covered the NHL for a living. Fantasy hockey should have added another layer of enjoyment that in no way diminished my original and long-standing love of the game. That's what *should* have happened. I think that's what happens with most fantasy sports players. That's what happened in the first two seasons that I played. But that's not what happened in 2006/'07.

What I liked about hockey from the first day I saw it more than fifty years ago is the speed, grace and artistry of play. That and the work of the goaltenders, who still draw a disproportionate amount of my attention when I go to a game. I recall the feeling I had as a ten-year old after I'd watched the first period of my first game, "Wow. I get to watch that *two* more times." Indeed, that was my feeling after every first period for about the next thirty years, or until sophisticated neutral zone defenses began turning the game into dump-and-chase and I began leaving games early to beat the traffic and going to bed after the second period of televised games. But I never stopped watching hockey completely until the end of my third year in a fantasy league, when the box scores suddenly became more important than the game. In this, I'm no doubt in a small minority. But I'm not alone.

"Did you ever play fantasy baseball?" I asked my friend Mark Leccese, a longtime Boston Red Sox season ticket holder and sometime catcher in baseball and softball. He said he had played in a fantasy league in the eighties, "but I quickly found the whole thing too time-consuming and it interfered with my general fandom. I just kind of gave it up. With the proliferation of information on the Internet maybe I should go back. But I still prefer just being a fan. And it irks me that (fantasy baseball) doesn't reward the skills I love the most: smart play, hitting the cut-off man, moving a runner over, having a good at-bat or a catcher calling a good game."

* * *

While in Italy in early March, and without a laptop computer, I'd scrambled each morning to find a copy of *The International Herald Tribune* so I could read NHL box scores already two days old. I flattered myself that missing one Monday trade deadline would cost me several places in the standings and I thought far more about the work of Roberto Luongo, another of my goalies, than about the works of Michelangelo.

When we arrived home from Italy I checked my fantasy team's standing before I unpacked my suitcase. I was No. 15, five places *higher* than I'd been when we left. So much for my role as management genius.

In the season's final few weeks I used the remainder of my twenty allowable roster changes, which briefly produced a net loss of twenty-one places until a last-week rally bounced me back into the top 30. I think I watched two games during the season's final three weeks: both involved Sidney Crosby. I did not sign up to play any post-season fantasy hockey, which I regard as a sucker bet because you're not only trying to pick players who will be successful but trying to find those players on teams that will go deep into the play-offs. Too many variables. Thus my fantasy season ended with the NHL's regular season.

On the first Sunday of post-season play there were two game telecasts, neither of which involved the Bruins, who finished out of the play-offs. No matter. I watched both games in their entirety notwithstanding that I had no stake in either. And I enjoyed those games as I had not enjoyed hockey since the early part of the season, back when reality still held the upper hand on fantasy.

"Nice to see you watching hockey again," Barb said as she walked through the living room.

I didn't have to ask why.

My check for $600 ($100 for being twenty-ninth overall, $500 for being No. 1 in December) arrived in mid-summer and I once again sent copies of the accompanying letter to various doubters and detractors. (Once a shift disturber always a shift disturber.) But I also decided that I wouldn't play fantasy hockey again. I don't ever again want to be as I was in the Sistine Chapel, distracted from the art.

SKATING THE RIDEAU CANAL

Health that mocks the doctor's rules.
—John Greenleaf Whittier,
"The Barefoot Boy"

We were cold, tired, hungry and skating in the dark through a snow squall on Ontario's Rideau Canal toward the lights of Ottawa, still a laborious mile away. I blamed Aurèle Joliat.

Most of the times that I'd read or heard about Joliat, an Ottawa native and legendary left wing on the Montreal Canadiens teams of the twenties and thirties, there was mention of his skating on the Rideau Canal, something he reportedly did until he was in his early eighties. Joliat died in 1986 at the age of eighty-four.

The vision of an old man skating through a city is poignant and romantic to me. In the mid-1960s a girlfriend and I skated many times on the pond in Boston's swank Public Garden, practically in the shadow of the old Ritz-Carlton. I laced up my skates, and hers, as was the chivalrous custom of the time, while sitting on the stone wall near the dock that in summer is the main base for the city's famous swan boats. I shot pucks off the support columns of the beautiful Haffenreffer pedestrian bridge. No one can do that any more because city officials—in what I suspect is a preemptive response to an increasingly litigious citizenry—drain the pond in winter. Instead of allowing free and unpatrolled skating in the Public Garden, the city has opened a skating rink about a half-mile away on the far less swank Boston Common. The new rink has lights, music, security guards, concession stands and admission fees. I don't skate there. I usually skate on a rink I have made in my backyard, where we also have lights and music but no admission fees or security guards and the only refreshment stand is the kitchen in which you can wear your skates as long as you're careful to step on the throw rugs we use to protect our floor from skate blades. Beer is in the fridge. Bottom right. No charge.

While I'd long known that one could skate on the Rideau Canal, I'd never been to Ottawa and might never have gone if it hadn't been for my wife, Barbara, the subsequent and long-term successor to the girlfriend of Public Garden memory.

"We have to do that sometime," Barb said when we were vacationing in Quebec and saw a painting of skaters on the Rideau. For me "sometime" often means "never." But Barb is a doer and so it was over a three-day mid-January Martin Luther King Jr. holiday weekend that we found ourselves driving north from Massachusetts toward the Ontario border early on a frigid Saturday morning. "What are those?" Barb asked, looking out the passenger-side front window toward a snowy farm field.

I snuck a quick look. "Coyotes," I said of the two animals loping with sinister lupine grace across the field toward the adjacent woods. It was the first and only time I've seen coyotes in the wild. "Tough day to be a coyote," I said, a reference to the cold.

"Tougher day to be a chicken if those dudes find you," said Barb, who'd spent several childhood summers on a farm in western Massachusetts. I thought about that over the next few miles. Both predators and prey were ultimately doomed. But in the meantime the farm animals would be sheltered, well fed and provided with veterinary care, while the coyotes would be free, free to starve or freeze to death to be sure, but free nonetheless. Unconfined. Forced to choose, I'd rather be a coyote.

In a minor way the matter of confinement was one of the reasons we were driving several hundred miles to skate on a canal. When we skate on our rink or on the aptly named Little Jennings Pond near our house, we're confined, our movement limited and prescribed by the configuration of boards or shore. I sometimes find it frustrating to skate on my rink. Just when a few more strides would generate more speed, it's time to turn. It's like driving a race car on a quarter-mile oval: you can never go full out; the straightaways are too short and the turns too frequent. When Barb skates alone on our rink, something she does frequently in the early evening, she carves a track of blade marks and deep gouges as she comes within inches of the boards, as if pushing the limits of her icy confinement. Barb skates with a short, choppy stride that can truly rip up a small sheet of ice. We were both looking forward to a long, free, straight-ahead skate as part of what we saw as a minor adventure and pleasant weekend.

* * *

Traffic was light, the border crossing fast and we were in our hotel by mid-afternoon. I'd booked us into the Fairmont Château Laurier because I saw on a map that it was within easy walking distance of the northern end of the exactly 4.4-mile (7-kilometer) skateable stretch of the Rideau. Our original plan had been to skate the Canal on Sunday, but with snow in the forecast and with a few hours of daylight remaining we decided to skate that afternoon. We skipped lunch and, dressed in lined nylon running suits and down parkas, hustled through the hotel lobby in which we saw at least a half-dozen people carrying skates. "Don't forget to take your boots with you," a woman at the desk told us and then immediately began backpedaling. "It's not that they're *likely* to be stolen but . . . well, there have been cases." I laughed because her warning reminded me of a time I'd played on a hockey team that practiced in the old Boston Arena, where our dressing room was occasionally broken into and money and clothes stolen while we were on the ice. Eventually we began putting our street clothes in our hockey bags and storing the bags on the bench. But it was a nuisance. "You think it's OK to leave our stuff here?" I'd asked teammate Dennis Griffin about the dressing room one night. "Only if you never want to see it again," he said.

Barb and I crossed Rideau Street and headed down an embankment toward the canal, which seemed to us to have a lot of skaters for so cold a day.

The only bad part of skating outdoors is putting on your skates. Our fingers were freezing as, one knee on the skate bag, we laced up and joined the hundreds of skaters in a river of humanity. There were skaters of all kinds: old smoothies, their long graceful strides carrying them easily over the ice; hockey players digging in harder than was necessary; children slipping and sliding while holding a parent's hand; and packs of teenage girls, a few of whom had the then fashionable slices of bare flat-bellied midriffs visible through unbuttoned coats, vanity trumping common sense. But most memorable were the red sleighs in which parents pushed children, some of whom were so bundled up that only their eyes shone through the swaddle of blankets. "Look. That's us someday," Barb said, nudging me and pointing to a sleigh containing what was apparently a grandmother and young grandchild wrapped in blankets and being pushed by two adults.

"I'd rather be the pusher than the pushee," I said but some of that was empty bravado. I was fifty-nine and Barb fifty-seven at the time. We'd become grandparents a few years earlier and I had lately begun to think of myself as getting old.

We put our boots in the two-handled canvas bag in which we'd carried our skates (it was a beach bag doubling as a skate bag) and began skating south. We were surprised at how fast and how easily we outdistanced the heavy concentration of skaters near the city and broke into the more open ice, where the canal turns from south to southwest. The only problem I had, at least at first, was the awkwardness of carrying the bag. It interfered with my stride and seemed to get heavier as we moved along. About a mile out of the city, we stopped at one of the small wooden refreshment stands to buy a local confection called a beavertail, a slab of fried dough topped with sugar and cinnamon, or, as the man in front of us in line said, "Fat, sugar and chocolate: what's not to like?"

We continued skating south, occasionally moving in behind one of the city plows that constantly scrape and clean the section of the canal that runs from the lock at the in-flow of the Ottawa River near Major's Hill Park south to another lock near a natural out-pouching of the canal called Dow's Lake. The entire Rideau Canal runs 126 miles (203 kilometers) and connects the Ottawa River with the city of Kingston, on Lake Ontario. Most of the canal follows the course of the Rideau River. The canal was conceived during the War of 1812 when Canada was still a British possession and, thus, England's ally in that two-and-a-half-year war against the fledgling United States. British military thinking was that, in the case of a future war between Canada and the United States, American forces would quickly take control of the St. Lawrence River, Canada's most important supply line. Thus the Rideau Canal was built as a safe route through the interior of Canada and with the intention that it be used to transport troops, munitions and supplies. The original cost of the canal, built between 1826 and 1832, was estimated at £169,000. But, in the great tradition of government construction projects, costs topped out at £829,804, then the largest single expenditure by Britain in North America. But the canal never became a route to a war zone. Instead its terminus at Kingston lies near what has become the world's longest undefended border. And the portion of the Rideau that runs through Ottawa is correctly known as the world's largest, not to mention most expensive, skating rink.

We'd skated, and dawdled, for about an hour when, maybe 300 yards ahead, we saw the lock marking the end of the skateable part of the canal. To our right was Dow's Lake, which is really more of a small bay with an island in the middle where there are a couple of restaurants. There was a pond hockey game going on to the right of the island. I hadn't brought a hockey stick, nor had I seen many on the canal. But there must have been some good skaters in this game because, even from a distance of several hundred yards, I could see their forms moving smoothly, swiftly and often at sharp angles to the ice. I couldn't see the puck, but, from the kaleidoscopic clusterings of players, I knew where the puck was and, often, which player had it. My tendency was to go watch a few minutes of the game. But it was beginning to get dark and a light snow had begun to fall. Thus, we decided to skate the shorter distance toward the lock so that we could say, rightly, that we'd skated the full skateable length of the canal. Then we'd head back to the city.

As soon as we made the turn I knew I was in trouble. We were skating north against a rising wind, and while Barb kept chugging along like The Little Engine That Could, my legs were tiring and the skate bag, once a mere inconvenience, was becoming an impediment. We didn't talk much on the way back.

We looked for the lights of oncoming plows and wordlessly moved into the clean ice in their wake. We'd gone perhaps a couple of miles when we saw a warming shack on the western shore of the pond.

"You want to take a break?" Barb asked.

"Got to make it a short one," I said, eager to sit down for a few minutes but anxious to get back to the city before the snow flurry became a storm.

We clomped into the crowded wooden shack and took the last two seats on the wooden bench against the east wall. I loosened my skates and immediately had what my childhood friends and I used to call "the numbies," these being a painful stinging of the feet, mainly your toes, caused by a combination of cold temperatures and skate laces tied so tightly that they restricted blood circulation. I kicked off my skates, straightened my legs and wiggled my toes just as I had so many times decades ago on the shores of skating ponds in my native Massachusetts.

Barbara simply sat there, a red-cheeked picture of robust health, as befitted a woman who has worked out an hour a day five to six days a week since 1979. "You OK?" she asked me.

"Got the numbies."

"Want me to take the bag?"

"Nah. I got it," I said. Pride deal. The fact is I wasn't OK. About an hour of what should have been easy skating had my legs and back hurting and my lungs struggling to make minimum payments on the oxygen debt. It was my own fault. I was carrying 217 pounds on a six-foot ectomorphic frame designed to carry perhaps 180. And too much of that weight was saddlebags of fat hanging on an ever expanding waistline.

We spent less than ten minutes in the shed before lacing up and heading back to the ice. It was darker now and the wind and snow were picking up. We saw the welcome lights of a southbound plow and headed for the cleared ice behind it. We didn't talk much as we skated the final mile toward the Ottawa skyline. I skated with my head down and the skate bag banging off of my tiring legs. Barb clip-clopped along, seemingly as fresh as when we'd started. We made it back to the north end of the canal, put our sweaty feet into freezing boots and walked stiff-legged back to our hotel.

"Have to admire Aurèle Joliat skating the canal in his eighties," I said as we waited for a pedestrian light to flash green.

"Who's Aurèle Joliat?" asked Barb, whose considerable hockey knowledge covers the roughly forty years from the arrival of Bobby Orr to the retirement of Wayne Gretzky. Anything since then is irrelevant and anything before then, except maybe for Rocket Richard and Gordie Howe, is a rumor shrouded in the mists of history. This is too bad because, as I told her, "if you played in the NHL you would have been Aurèle Joliat."

"I would've been Pie McKenzie," she said of the spunky ex-Bruins winger Johnny "Pie" McKenzie, who is still Barb's all-time favorite player. Any sport. Any era.

I explained that Joliat and McKenzie were the same type of player, little guys with short tempers and big hearts. That Barb, the career penalty minutes leader on our backyard rink, was the same *type* of person went, prudently and diplomatically, without saying. (I haven't made it through forty years of marriage by taking stupid penalties.)

* * *

Aurèle Emile Joliat was born in Ottawa on August 29, 1901. He began his athletic career as a fullback and kicker with the Ottawa Rough Riders, but a broken leg prompted him to give up football for hockey. He skated for Ottawa's New Edinburghs, a club team, before heading west to find work in the wheat fields of Saskatchewan. He was playing hockey for the Saskatoon Sheiks in 1922 when he got traded to the Montreal Canadiens for the popular and once great Newsy Lalonde. Joliat rode the Montreal bench for most of his first season. But in 1923 he was teamed with then newcomer Howie Morenz, and the two linemates, together with right wing Billy Boucher, skated themselves to immortality. Morenz was the swift-skating goal-scoring machine. Joliat, almost as fast as Morenz, was a slick play maker, consistent goal scorer and relentless back-checker. Joliat weighed 160 pounds when he first joined the Canadiens, but he quickly brought that down to about 130, an astonishing loss of almost 20 percent of his body weight, thus improving his speed and endurance. Joliat was so light and small that he should have been run out of NHL rinks. But you can't hit what you can't catch, and the man fans nicknamed the "Mighty Atom" and the "Little Giant" was quick and elusive. Joliat played wearing a black cap that hid a bald spot. Opponents sometimes pulled off the hat, an act of schoolyard-type bullying that the feisty Joliat immediately repaid with hacks, slashes and trips. Joliat was also the forward most likely to be the first man hustling back on defense. It isn't a stretch to say Aurèle Joliat's defensive play foreshadowed the defensive scheme that would later become known as the left-wing lock. Joliat won the Hart Trophy as the NHL's most valuable player in 1934. He retired in 1938, the season after his best friend, Morenz, died of complications resulting from a broken leg sustained in a hockey game. Forty-six years later, Joliat came back to the Forum for one last skate. It was a terrible mistake, or so I and many others long thought.

As part of their seventy-fifth anniversary in 1984, the Canadiens invited the stars from the team's storied past to a reunion at the Forum. Those who came included the Rocket, Doug Harvey, Dickie Moore, Jean Béliveau, and a constellation of stars unmatched by any other team in hockey. The last player to be introduced to the crowd was then eighty-one-year-old Aurèle Joliat. Instead of simply stepping out in street shoes onto the red carpet, Joliat had decided he would burst out of the tunnel, skate onto the ice, wave his hat to the adoring crowd, then stickhandle a puck toward the far goal. But when the once Mighty Atom hit the ice, he promptly fell, sending what veteran Montreal *Gazette* hockey writer Red Fisher recalls as "an embarrassed buzz" through the crowd. Joliat jumped to his feet and resumed skating. But he caught a skate blade on the red carpet and fell again. Harder. He got up slower this time and the moment was ruined. "It was a sad thing to see," Claude Mouton, the late Montreal public address announcer, told me as he stared at the press room floor and shook his head while describing the incident to me a few weeks after it happened.

I at first thought it was pride, not the red carpet, that had sent Joliat tumbling. Hubris, I thought, self-deceiving vanity, the deadly seducer of aging athletes. I briefly envisioned an aging Willie Mays staggering around under fly balls in the New York Mets outfield. I pitied Joliat and felt embarrassed for him. But that was before I got stood up at the blue line of mortality.

* * *

Barb and I spent a cold, sunny Sunday exploring Ottawa's ByWard Market, a twenty-four-block grid of shops and restaurants, part of which was laid out in 1826 by Colonel John By, the British army officer who supervised the building of the Rideau Canal. Ottawa was called By Town until 1855.

We ducked into a restaurant, where I ordered a chicken Caesar salad and a diet Coke. "Got to lose some weight," I said, recalling with embarrassment my skating struggles of the previous day.

For a few months I made a half-hearted effort to eat smarter and to skate harder on the backyard rink. But my resolve melted with our ice and I soon returned to my sedentary and unhealthy ways. Or I did until I got what I still think of as The Big Scare. It was about two years after Barb and I had skated the canal that we attended a family party where Barb's niece Kathy Maloney, a registered nurse, was amusing her many young nieces and nephews by taking their blood pressure. "Put that blood pressure cuff on me. I'll shoot you a double triple," I said, knowing my blood pressure tended to be high. What I didn't know is that I would put up numbers that belonged in a National Basketball Association All-Star game.

"You're a ticking time bomb," Kathy said as she looked at a reading I recall as being 200 over 115. "You're a heart attack waiting to happen. And a candidate for a stroke." That got my attention. It got Barb's too, but she only raised her eyes to heaven. Barb is a registered nurse too, and one in possession of a blood pressure cuff, but she had years ago given up urging me to see doctors more often than I do, which is almost never except for a couple of times I've needed stitches or a broken bone set.

"What do I do?" I asked Kathy.

"Lose ten pounds. And get some blood pressure pills," she said.

I was scared enough to break form. I didn't see a doctor, but I did see a nurse practitioner, who, on June 22, 2006, wrote me a prescription for blood pressure pills. I came home with a plastic bottle of something called Atenolol. I opened the bottle and shook one pill, a tiny white jobbie, into my hand. I reached for one of the bottled waters we keep on the kitchen counter. Then I stopped. I stared at the pill, which I no longer saw as a helpful drug but as my first step down the slippery slope I'd watched elderly aunts and uncles descend, one by one falling into an abyss, where one prescription was followed by another until there were so many pills that a relative or visiting nurse had to place them in compartmentalized plastic boxes. I recalled my late Aunt Marie's plastic box, seven rows of compartments, one for each day of the week; and three compartments per row, one for morning, afternoon and evening. Some of the morning boxes contained five or six pills. You could look at that as the wonders of modern pharmacology prolonging a person's life and, thus, a person's possibilities. But that's not how I looked at it. I saw and still see that little pill as the first step toward a kind of chemical confinement.

I dumped my blood pressure pill back in the bottle, put the bottle in my sock drawer and headed for the local high school track. That was and remains an irrational decision. I won't try to defend it because it's indefensible. I should view modern medicine as my ally in the battle against the encroachments of age and illness and as a means of extending life and its possibilities. Taking a blood pressure pill is easy and painless. Many of my friends and relatives do it. I wouldn't want to see them stop. I just didn't want to start. I can't explain my thinking, but I can explain my feelings. I was angry and resolved. Age was hitting me. I would hit back. Maybe that was anger trumping fear. Or maybe it's a hockey thing. Or maybe I'd just rather be the coyote.

I didn't run or jog on those first days on the track. I didn't dare to. I walked. And kept walking. Through the mid-summer heat of July and August and on into September and October I circled that track, often using the time to think about a novel I was writing. I kept walking, and eventually jogging, until snow and ice covered the track and rendered it unusable. But by that time my backyard rink was open and I was skating longer and harder than I had in years, doing stops and starts as if driven by an inner Herb Brooks, "Again. Again." When the track reopened I was back on it, still walking more than I ran but running more than I used to.

The pounds disappeared and Barb's blood pressure cuff, which she seemed more willing to use if it promised to deliver improving numbers, showed progress. Slowly, and without drugs, my blood pressure dropped to a low of 126 over 82, still high but not as dangerously high as it had been. Meanwhile I had dropped my weight from 217 to 183 pounds, a Joliat-like reduction. Unlike Joliat I wasn't trying to play for the Canadiens: I was trying to stay on the top side of the ice. It was at dinner on New Year's Eve of 2006, New Year's Eve being a night when we stay home to review the old year and plan for the new one, that Barb and I decided we'd skate the Rideau Canal once more.

We planned to again take advantage of the three-day Martin Luther King Jr. weekend, but an unusually warm winter kept the Rideau, and our backyard rink, un-skateable until February. The canal didn't open for skating until the first weekend in February, barely in time for Ottawa's annual Winterlude, a mid-winter festival of music, art, ice sculpture and, of course, skating on the canal.

Such is the popularity of Winterlude that we couldn't get a room at the Château Laurier, but we managed to get into the Westin Hotel, which we were delighted to discover is even closer to the northernmost end of the canal. This time we'd made a couple of changes that we recommend for anyone planning to skate the Rideau: (1) we brought a backpack in which to carry our footwear, and (2) we wore lightweight sneakers instead of the heavy boots we'd burdened ourselves with on our first skate.

Barb went into a wooden shack to put on her skates while I sat on the edge of the shack's deck and laced up with far greater ease than I had three years and thirty-four pounds earlier. Our adventure got off to a shaky start when Barb, emerging from the shack, slipped and fell hard, her skate blades out in front of her, the right blade narrowly missing my left arm and the left blade just as narrowly missing the right arm of a woman who was also sitting on the deck.

"Are you OK?" the woman and I asked almost simultaneously.

"I'm fine," Barb said, jumping to her feet and taking a few strides away from the deck. I put our sneakers in the backpack and headed out into a throng of skaters far more numerous than we'd encountered the first time we'd skated the canal. Another tip: if you have a choice, don't skate the Rideau Canal on a weekend afternoon during Winterlude.

We'd skated about 500 yards when Barb veered too close to the bad ice nearest the shore and her right blade crunched through a soft spot. She fell again. Bounced up again.

"You OK?"

"Fine," she said, laughing.

My weight loss made this skate a breeze for me. About halfway down the canal we stopped at a faux Indian encampment and shared a hot chocolate. And this time when we approached the end of the canal, we turned west and skated around Dow's Lake before heading back toward the city.

Skating in daylight and without the burden of fatigue, I noticed things I hadn't noticed before. I was surprised at the amount of French spoken by other skaters. Ottawa is located near the Ontario/Quebec border and one-sixth of the city's residents are francophone. But that fraction seemed nearer one-fourth among the skaters on the Rideau. I was also surprised to see almost as many Montreal Canadiens jerseys and hats as jerseys and hats of the hometown Ottawa Senators. In our entire skate I saw only one person, a boy of about ten, wearing a Toronto Maple Leafs shirt.

I was a few yards ahead of Barb when I heard a crunch and a thud. I turned to see Barb sprawled face-first on the ice, skaters swerving around her. She'd hit another bad patch of ice, broken through and come down on her right knee. Hard. She got up on her left knee and for a second or two looked like a fighter about to take an eight count. Then she bounced up, smiling, and again skating straight ahead in her inimitable style. The purpose-driven wife. I've long admired Barb's physical and mental resilience. And lately that's led me to wonder why I pitied, rather than admired, Aurèle Joliat. Sure, he did a vain and showy-offy thing. And he paid for it. But is the significance and enduring memory to be that he fell twice? Or that he got up twice?

I recalled something my friend Steve Dryden, then editor of *The Hockey News,* now a producer for the TSN television network, had said to me several years ago, something to the effect that reaction to Joliat's falling was "overblown." I recently asked Steve exactly what he'd meant. "I was miffed that Joliat didn't have more support [from fans] during his skate at the Forum," was Steve's emailed reply. "As I recall he fell twice and both times got up and carried on as though nothing had happened." Steve said he "applauded his [Joliat's] spunky attitude."

In retrospect so do I. Hubris aside, and there was probably a lot of it to push aside, I applaud the heart of an octogenarian even *trying* to do what Joliat almost did. The Little Giant didn't want to go quietly into that good night. Good for him. I choose to remember Aurèle Joliat as the man who got up, not the man who went down.

* * *

Even with our hot chocolate break, Barb and I finished our skate in an effortless eighty-five minutes. And this time I could have skated it again. Easily.

We were almost back to our hotel when, on Rideau Street, we walked past a pub called the Elephant and Castle. Well, we *almost* walked past it.

"You want to grab a beer?" Barb said.

In my fight to lose weight I'd almost given up beer. The weekly six-pack I used to buy when grocery shopping has become the *monthly* six-pack. But, yes, after skating the Rideau Canal I wanted a beer. We got the last available table in the pub, I dropped our skate bag on the floor and grabbed a menu, but before I could read it a waitress appeared.

"What's the soup?" Barb asked.

"Potato and bacon," the waitress said.

"Oooooh, potato soup," said Barb, who is half Irish and for whom the potato, baked, mashed, roasted, au gratin, scalloped, you name it, is the glittering jewel beckoning atop the apex of the food pyramid. We each ordered a Stella Artois draft and a bowl of potato and bacon soup.

"Here's to us," Barb said, raising her glass.

"Us and Aurèle Joliat," I said, clinking my glass against hers. I said I'd had a lot more fun on our second skate than I'd had on the first and that skating the Rideau "is something we should do every two or three years."

"Fine with me," she said.

Then I pushed it. "You think we could skate it into our eighties?" I asked.

"You'll be eighty, I'll only be seventy-eight," she said.

"But do you think we could?"

"No," she said, and she said it with blunt authority. Besides being a registered nurse, Barb is also a licensed social worker in which capacity she works at a local senior center. Four days a week she helps the aged and aging. She knows that exercise and a healthy diet are rearguard actions that can delay, but won't stop, the deadly advance of age. In the end we're like the Spartans at Thermopylae, fighting a noble fight in the face of crushingly certain finality.

I knew Barb was right. Actuarial tables, observation and the entire history of humankind tell me that two people seventy-eight and eighty are unlikely to be skating at all much less skating the Rideau Canal. But that the goal is unlikely doesn't make it unworthy.

"Let's call it our *reach* goal," I said.

"Fine," she said, that being a kind of code word Barb uses to indicate that a topic has been exhausted or that she's lost interest in the conversation. But this time I ran through the indicator.

"If I couldn't skate the canal but you could, would you skate it alone?" I asked.

She thought about that for a minute. "No. It's something to be shared," she said.

"Let's skate it for as long as we can and if we can skate when

I'm eighty let's give it a shot. Only eighteen more years. And it's not like we'd have to skate all the way to the end, right?"

Barb froze and stared at me, a spoonful of potato and bacon soup halfway to her mouth. "And back," she said.

We left Ottawa early Sunday morning, driving south through Montreal on into Vermont, then southeast to Massachusetts. A minute or two after leaving the hotel we were on Colonel By Drive, which runs along the east bank of the Rideau Canal. There were only a few skaters on the ice, including a man on long-bladed speed skates, his arms behind him and the tassel of his stocking cap bouncing off his back as he fairly flew down the most inviting sheet of open ice I've ever seen. "Next time let's skate early on Sunday morning," I said.

"You want to stop and skate now?" Barb asked.

I did want to skate, but I also wanted to get home before dark, so I kept driving. Barb fell asleep. As I settled into my long-distance driving mode I thought again about the possibility of pulling an Aurèle Joliat and skating the Canal at age eighty. I thought about skating it with Barb and I thought about skating it alone. I found both thoughts poignant and romantic.

NEW SKATES

Old friends are best. King James used to call
for his old shoes; they were easiest for his feet.
—John Sheldon, "Table Talk"

The winter of 2006/'07 came late to New England, then apologized
for its tardiness by bringing us a rare gift, black ice in February.
Black ice, the perfectly transparent ice that gets its color and
name from the mucky pond water below it, usually belongs to
December or early January. By late January, in a typical year, the
once rock-hard black ice is soft and gray from the admixture
of snow and slush. By February that ice is usually inaccessible,
buried under a layer of snow or pockmarked with so many
footprints as to render it un-skateable. It was to take advantage
of this rare late-season black ice that on a Sunday afternoon in
2007 I grabbed my skate bag and a hockey stick and headed for
Little Jennings Pond a quarter-mile from my house.

About a dozen kids in the ten- to fourteen-year age range and two adult men were there ahead of me. A few of the kids had laced up and commandeered the best section of ice for what was obviously going to be a hockey game. But the two men and most of the kids were still in the process of putting on their skates. I walked a few yards onto the ice, plopped down my skate bag and pulled out my skates. At the top and edges of my field of vision I saw what I expected to see—the sidelong glances of the kids and adults, looks that seemed to say: "What in the world are those?" In this case "those" were my twenty-two-year-old Micron Quadra-Flexes, a style of skate worn in the 1980s by a handful of NHL players—Ken "Rat" Linseman and Charlie Simmer come immediately to mind—but rarely seen in the past two decades and, judging from some of the looks they got, comically ancient to the current generation of skaters.

The skate is of two-piece construction: a black plastic lower boot connects by a hinge to a gray plastic upper section that encases the skater's ankle. The skate is lined with a removable padded bootie, the softness and warmth of which makes the old Quadra-Flex a great skate for the diminishing number of us who do most of our skating outdoors. But that doesn't make it any less embarrassing to be seen in.

I'd been seeing those sidelong glances more frequently: once at the local town rink when I took my grandson skating, again when I skated Ottawa's Rideau Canal, and again almost every time a guest skates on my backyard rink for the first time. We'll be lacing up in my kitchen and I'll see "the look" made up of four parts curiosity and one part disdain. Most guests are too polite to say anything. Doc Kelly isn't most guests.

"When are you going to break down and buy new skates?" Doc asked in early March of 2006 as we were putting on our skates in my kitchen. Doc, a native New Englander and now headmaster of a private school in Texas, was in Boston on business and had come to my house to skate on my rink, something he does every time he comes to Massachusetts in the winter. That Doc would disparage my skates is remarkable only when you consider that his skates are thirteen years older than mine.

"Why'd you carry those relics all the way to Texas?" I asked in an effort to change the subject from my skates to his.

"Because they're my skates," he said. "Besides, they're Tacks." It was the latter comment that ended the discussion. Doc's skates are the all-leather Tackaberrys of a style made famous not by Ken Linseman and Charlie Simmer but by Bobby Orr and Gordie Howe. When Doc pulls out his vintage Tacks, it's like a guy driving into the company parking lot in an antique Rolls-Royce. When I pull out my rusting-riveted, frayed-laced, beaten-up Quadra-Flexes, I'm like the guy rumbling into the parking lot in a clapped-out 1968 Plymouth Road Runner, nice in its day, *but . . .*

Months after his March 2006 visit, Doc sent me a letter in which he wrote of his skates:

I have kept the old Tacks mainly because I don't skate enough to warrant new ones (but also) because they fit. My feet know them and adjust to them quickly even when I haven't worn them for awhile. I can count on them. When I cut I know they'll be there for me.

I began thinking of the difference between the way hockey players feel about our sticks versus our skates: we're meticulous about our sticks but are literally and figuratively attached to our skates. I think this is similar to a baseball player's feelings about his bat and his glove. As my friend Mark Leccese, a baseball catcher from Little League to an Over-40 league, once told me: "Your bat is a date. Your glove is your wife." Same thing with sticks and skates.

But I never took a for-better-or-worse vow with my skates and so it was on a hot day in the summer of 2006 that I walked into a big-box sporting goods store intending to buy a new pair of skates.

I looked at the display models mounted on stands above stacks of boxes. I pulled out two boxes labeled size 10, went to a nearby chair and slipped my foot into one of the skates. The skate was so stiff and inflexible that I may as well have had my foot in a bench vise.

"Can I help you?" asked a young man who wore a plastic name tag identifying him as a Sales Associate.

"Do you have anything with a little flexibility to it?" I asked.

"Ahh, I think they're all pretty much the same," he said in a tone combining so much boredom and lack of self-assurance as to make me think that what Mr. Sales Associate didn't know about skates was well worth knowing.

"That's OK. I'll just try on a few," I said, this seeming to come as a relief to Mr. Sales Associate, who had begun edging toward the golf department like a base runner preparing to steal second.

But I didn't try on more skates. I put the boxes back on the shelf, drove home and squeezed yet another season out of my Microns.

I could handle the scornful curiosity of other skaters. But late in the winter of 2007, I began thinking that my skates were ready to break. The big hinges holding the upper part of the boot to the lower were rusting, some eyelets looked ready to pop, the rust on the rivets and along the sides of the blades was getting darker and looking more corrosive. And the right boot made an ominous squeaking sound when I pulled the laces tight.

There would be no backing out this time. On May 23, 2007, I tore a blank check out of my checkbook, entered the date, the check number and "Natick Outdoor Store" in my ledger, I could fill in the amount when I knew it. I headed to what has become a rarity on the North American commercial landscape: an independent sporting goods store located in what we townies call "downtown" and staffed by people who know what they're talking about.

I was looking at a wall filled with display model skates when I was approached by a young man who was not wearing a name tag but who later introduced himself as Michael Caulfield. He asked if he could help me. "Trying to find something flexible in a size 10," I said.

"Let me measure your foot," he said.

"That's OK. I'm a size 11 shoe and a size 10 skate," I said, the subtext of which statement was to let him know that I knew one's skate size is always smaller than one's shoe size.

"Let's just check," he said, putting a metal foot-measuring device on the floor. I kicked off my loafers and put my right foot in the device. He slid a bar onto my toe. I saw the reading, size 11. He measured my left foot. Also size 11. Vindication.

"Nine and a half," said Michael Caulfield.

"I take a 10. Really," I said, but by then Caulfield was heading toward the stockroom. He came back with two boxes: two different brands of skates, both size 9½. I put one brand on my left foot and one on my right. They fit perfectly. They also fit painfully. The size was right, but the iron inflexibility, the pressing in of the metal-stiff boot against the various bone outcroppings and other oddities of my feet, was uncomfortable. The boots were so stiff I could barely bend the sides out far enough so that I could run the laces through the eyelets. I stood up and walked around on a large rubber floor mat. After a minute or so of walking, the skate on my left foot, a Nike/Bauer Supreme (albeit not the top-of-the-line Supreme of the 1970s and '80s), began to feel slightly more comfortable. I was about to say I'd take the Bauers when I did something uncharacteristic. I hesitated. I hemmed. I hawed. I tried on more skates. I stalled. I acted in a way I never act in a store. Put me in front of a menu, a wine list or even a stack of doughnut trays and I call out my decision with the confidence of a quarterback calling a play. Barbara says I'd rather be wrong than indecisive. She's mostly right. But this time I couldn't pull the trigger. Caulfield bailed me out.

"We've got a big shipment of skates due in next week. Let me put the Bauers aside for you," he said, writing my name on a pad of paper, "and next week come in and see what else we've got."

I thanked him and left the store, happy and at least momentarily relieved. I used the blank check at the grocery store where

I did our weekly shopping (and made my meat, fish and produce selections with the cocksure decisiveness of a Tom Brady).

The following Thursday I was to return to the sporting goods store and complete my purchase of new skates. But I didn't. Instead I drove to Ottawa to attend an NHL-sponsored reunion of the six surviving members of the Montreal Canadiens dynasty that won five Stanley Cups in a row from 1956 to 1960, a feat they accomplished while wearing all-leather Tackaberrys. Before leaving town I stopped briefly at the Outdoor Store. I told Michael Caulfield I'd return the following week. The truth is I could have afforded the half-hour or so it would have taken to try on the skates again, get them sharpened and pay for them. I was, in fact, leaving for Ottawa. But I was also stalling.

I returned to the store the following Tuesday to find that Caulfield was off duty, his place taken by hockey department head Peter Brandwein, a man who knows how to close a sale.

"Got your skates right here," said Brandwein, pulling a black box with the Nike swoosh logo and the Bauer name off a shelf beside his desk.

"Has the new shipment come in? Thought I might try something else," I said.

"Sure. But why don't you try these first," he said.

I'd forgotten to wear socks, so I bought a pair of thin white cotton socks and put on the skates. They laced up easier this time and seemed to feel better. "Sold," I said, with more resignation than confidence.

"You got about a half-hour? It'll take us that long to fit and sharpen these," said Brandwein.

"Fit them? They already fit," I said.

"No. We heat-mold them to your feet," said Brandwein, describing what I now understand is a common process but one that was technologically bewildering to me, a skater who since childhood had broken in new skates by skating in them.

Brandwein pulled the laces and insoles out of the boots and put the skates into something called a Bauer Thermal Fit Unit, which looked to me like a small toaster oven. It took eight minutes for the skates to heat up to 180 degrees. Brandwein then put the insoles and laces back in the skates. "Lace 'em up good and tight," he said.

I didn't want to lace them up at all. I have a peculiar aversion to anything hot and had to touch the boot to satisfy myself that it wouldn't burn me. I then laced on the skates, whereupon Brandwein told me I had to sit or stand (I stood) in the skates for twenty minutes while the boots cooled down and molded themselves to my feet. I mentioned that the warm skates felt good. "Yeah, it feels sort of therapeutic," said Brandwein. "Had a customer last year who wanted to come back every week. Had arthritis or something."

While my skates cooled, I talked shop with Brandwein. "Feel these," he said taking three top-of-the-line skates, an Easton Synergy, a Nike/Bauer Vapor xxx and a CCM Vector 10.0, off a wall display rack. The skates I was wearing, a midline skate, were light, but the top-end skates were lighter. "If a kid's playing high school hockey and skating every day, I'll put him in one of these," said Brandwein of the high-end skates, all bearing price tags north of $400. "But for the recreational skater, I'll try to put him in something like you have. Those skates will last you, …" and here Peter Brandwein diplomatically hit the brakes, apparently not knowing how to finish the thought. I finished it for him. "They'll last me the rest of my life," I said, laughing to ease what I thought was a little embarrassment.

I had Brandwein put a goalie radius on my blade. I'm used to—and probably need—a lot of blade on the ice. "Ever put a goalie radius on a regular skate before?" I asked Brandwein. His answer surprised me.

"Little kids' skates," he said. "To give kids more stability when they're learning to skate."

I thought it was a great idea and made a mental note to do this for my grandchildren.

The next day I took my new skates to the town rink for the morning public skating session. I also brought my old skates, just in case.

"Three bucks," said an attendant seated at a card table at the glass door that opened to the ice surface. All I had were $20 bills and, because I was the second skater there, the attendant didn't have change. He sighed and rose slowly from his folding metal chair, obviously unhappy about having to walk back to the office to get change. I started walking with him. We'd gone only a few steps when he turned and said. "How old are you?"

"Sixty-three," I said.

"Senior citizens skate free," he said and returned to his chair.

I said "thanks" but I didn't mean it. It was the first time

anyone had taken me for, much less actually called me, a senior citizen. I don't feel old and when I skate I feel positively boyish. I would sooner have given the man the twenty and told him to keep the change than to have been reminded that I, unlike my new skates, have more yesterdays than tomorrows.

I laced up the new skates and walked toward the door leading to the ice. Is there one among us who, while toddling along a rubber mat toward a rink, doesn't, in some deep secret recess of his mind, think of himself as a "real" NHL player stepping out for a "real" game?

* * *

I once coached varsity hockey at a nearby private school, where, during a brief break in a practice, an assistant coach pointed to a corner of the rink, the same one on which I was now about to try my new skates. There, three of our better players had opened the door leading to the dressing room, stepped briefly off the ice, then, one at a time, turned and jogged back toward the open door and jumped through it, fairly exploding onto the ice surface.

"Would you go see what that's all about?" I asked the assistant coach who returned a moment later with the answer.

"They say they're practicing their Beanpot entrances," he said, laughing.

The Beanpot Hockey Tournament is a popular competition among Boston College, Boston University, Harvard and Northeastern, held annually at a sold-out Boston Garden. Herein bands play, 17,565 fans cheer and players charge onto the ice with football-like ferocity. Years later I was at the Boston Garden when one of those former high school players, a Boston University defenseman, skated out for his first Beanpot game. I found his entrance smooth and stylish with only a trace element of self-consciousness.

* * *

For once I didn't feel like a player or even an adequate skater as I headed for the ice in my new skates. I felt like a new skater, anxious and uncertain. There would be no Beanpot entrance. I held onto the dasher board and stepped slowly, gingerly, onto the ice. I didn't even take a stride. I glided a few feet, with my arms held out for balance, much as they must have been more than a half-century ago when I skated for the first time. By now several figure skaters were on the ice. I admire figure skaters because they're alone. But in those first few minutes on new blades among good skaters I felt, and must have looked, like a rank novice.

The boots felt good. But the blades sat on the ice differently than did the blades on my old skates. There wasn't quite as much blade behind the heel and for a minute or two, I had the feeling I might fall backward. But by the second lap around the rink I was cross-cutting on turns and by the third lap I was turning and skating backwards, albeit awkwardly and still with that lurking fear of falling. The best skating, like the best golfing, place kicking or sex, is a product of relaxed confidence. I was neither relaxed nor confident as I turned those first few laps.

I've always felt sorry for those four-, five- and six-year olds first learning to skate, struggling to keep up with their peers and not be embarrassed in front of their coffee-sipping parents staring through puck-smudged glass or in front of coaches who, no matter how encouraging, are also judging. But if what I used to feel was compassion, what I now feel is empathy. I'm embarrassed to be skating so tentatively and poorly. I skate for twenty minutes, the last five of which are acceptable as I begin to adjust to the blades and regain a modicum of confidence.

When I get home I store my new and old skates and Barbara's three-year-old skates in one of the vacant upstairs bedrooms rather than in the basement, where dampness would further corrode the blades and rivets. A good move, I think—and only twenty-three years too late.

* * *

That evening I received an email from my friend Gerry Hailer who, even at fifty-two, is still playing goal, and playing it well, in a senior hockey league. His sons, Nick and Peter, are also goalies, and Gerry was writing me to tell me about Nick's summer hockey schedule. In my emailed reply I casually mentioned that I'd just tried out my new skates and that no one had mistaken me for Mario Lemieux. It was a throwaway remark to which I neither sought nor expected a reply. But I got one. When I logged on to my computer the next morning, it was to find that Gerry had emailed me an impromptu essay on new skates:

New skates are like new cars, aren't they? It takes us awhile to get over the old ones even though the new ones are better. We all have a history with, and a physical as well as psychological attachment to, our skates. You've got to believe in them, they've got to feel like an extension of your feet and legs, like you're not even aware of them [and yet] you trust them so much.

We love our skates or we search until we find skates we love. It's that critical to success and survival on the ice. Sticks come and go. Skates come and stay. As for your new skates, you'll grow into them psychologically and then they'll become yours.

* * *

I returned to the town rink the following week. I handed three $1 bills to the attendant. "I'll feel better if I pay," I said.

I skated better this time. Not as well as I would have skated in my old Microns, which I'd left home, but with less self-consciousness. A Frankie Valli song, "Can't Take My Eyes Off You," came over the rink's sound system and I found myself skating to the music while maintaining the charade that I was not actually *trying* to skate to the music. I looked around the rink and realized I was the only skater old enough to have heard the song when it charted in 1967.

I came home and put my new skates back in my son's old upstairs room beside my old skates. I thought briefly of throwing away my old skates. But I've kept them, ostensibly as loaners for guests who might want to skate on my backyard rink. The real reason is that they're my skates.

PASSING THE TORCH

Every tradition grows more venerable
The more remote is its origin.
—Friedrich Wilhelm Nietzsche

On the evening of Saturday, November 11, 2006, my grandson Demetre became the fifth generation of my family to see a Bruins game. I held his hand as I led him toward a balcony passageway that gave him his first wide-eyed look at the 17,565-seat TD Banknorth Garden, successor to the original Boston Garden, where I had seen my first game fifty-one seasons earlier. Demetre's and my arrival meant that there was now an unbroken chain that stretched back to my paternal grandmother and that included my father, me, my son and daughter, and now the blond-haired boy standing beside me momentarily stopped in his tracks—as I had once been—by the panorama of a nearly-empty arena: the steppes of seats sweeping down to a beckoning plain of ice with its painted lines and huge black-spoked *B* in the middle. That icy stage and its predecessors, at the first Boston Garden and, before that, at the Boston Arena, where successive generations of my family cheered for a pantheon of Bruins immortals beginning with Eddie Shore and continuing to Milt Schmidt, Bobby Orr, Ray Bourque and, on this night, though we didn't yet know it, to Patrice Bergeron.

"You've been waiting seven years for this, Dad," my daughter Tracey, Demetre's mother, said to me on the afternoon of the game when we found ourselves alone in the kitchen. "How do you feel?"

"Like I was starting in goal," I said.

"What are you so worried about?"

"I've never taken him anywhere by myself except Dunkin' Donuts," I said.

"You took him to the fair," she said. Alas, she hadn't forgotten.

Three years earlier I had indeed taken my grandson to a county fair in Maine. It was not a day likely to bring about my enshrinement in a Grandparents' Hall of Fame.

The Cumberland County Fairgrounds lie about a mile from my grandson's house. I'd driven the 135 miles from my home in Massachusetts to take then four-year-old Demetre to the fair. I did it because it seemed like a grandfatherly thing to do and for the more practical reason that I am the family member least likely to get sick accompanying him on rides like the Tilt-A-Whirl, the flying cups and saucers or other such rapidly spinning, sphincter-tightening alleged amusements.

The Ferris wheel was my undoing. Demetre and I were at the top of the wheel when it stopped to discharge and take on passengers. I was enjoying the view of late-September foliage when Demetre looked to his left and spotted a racetrack.

"What's that, Grandpa Jack?" he asked.

"A race track," I said.

"They have car racing here?"

"Horse racing," I said.

He thought about that for a while. "Can we go see?" he said.

When we got off the Ferris wheel we walked to the main gate of the track's grandstand. I reached for my wallet, but the man at the gate handed me a program and waved us through. It was about fifteen minutes before the start of the afternoon's harness racing card. We walked up to the fence to watch the trotters working out. This is where I made my mistake.

"You know, you can bet on these races," I said.

"What's bet?"

"If you guess which horse wins the race, you can win money."

"How many tickets does that take?" he asked, obviously thinking that the races worked the same as the amusement rides.

"It takes money. Two dollars," I said.

Demetre reached into his pocket and pulled out a mangled dollar bill. "I have $1," he said.

I said I had another dollar and that he could pick the horse we'd bet on. I read him the names from the program. I forget the full name of the horse, but part of it was a girl's name. I think it was Heather. The horse was a prohibitive favorite. "This Heather horse is probably going to win," I said.

Demetre was silent for a minute. "Think we should bet on old Heather?" I said trying to prompt his agreement.

"Heather at school bit me," he said. "That wasn't nice." It sounded improbable, but I later learned from my daughter that at preschool a girl named Heather had in fact bitten him on the shoulder in a squabble over a toy. "He might feel differently about that in sixteen years or so," I'd said to Tracey, who glared at me. Tracey glares like Clint Eastwood.

So Heather was out. Instead my grandson picked an 18-to-1 shot with a name he liked. The horse came in and paid $30-something. Then he picked the winner of the second race. Same system. Together we picked the winner of the third race and were now up more than $50 for the day. I worried that my grandson might think the racetrack was an ATM. I wanted him to lose a race before we left. We lost the fourth race, which seemed not to bother him at all. We split our winnings—about $25 each—and headed for the car and the short drive home.

"What'll you do with your money?" I asked.

"Give it to Mama to put in the bank," he said.

We went on to construct a scenario where he would some-day have enough money to buy a car and drive his friends to school. "I'd drive Luke and Dylan and Hunter," he said.

"Not Heather?"

"Heather's not nice."

We pulled up to my daughter's house. As soon as I'd un-buckled him from his car seat, my grandson went bounding into the kitchen brandishing his fistful of bills. "Look at this, Mama," he yelled.

"Where did you get that, Demetre?" she asked.

"At the horse races with Grandpa Jack," he said, just as I stepped through the door in time to catch another squinty-eyed glare from my daughter. The immediately ensuing lecture took a strange form. Instead of talking directly to me, Tracey turned back to the stove, where she'd been preparing dinner, and, in a sing-songy rhetorical soliloquy, inquired: "And what was Grandpa Jack thinking? . . . Or *was* Grandpa Jack thinking? . . . And exactly what message did Grandpa Jack think he was sending? . . . What kind of example was he setting?"

I turtled. Said nothing. Veteran's move.

After my trip to the fair, I seemed to be on a kind of supervised probation. When I took Demetre to a Quebec Major Junior Hockey League game in Lewiston, Maine, where we saw future NHL star Sidney Crosby, who was then with the Rimouski Oceanic, play against the hometown Lewiston Maineiacs, I found myself accompanied by Tracey, her husband, Maurice, and my wife, Barbara. Same thing when I took Demetre to a Portland Sea Dogs AA baseball game that summer. And the next. Clearly I was a man who had not mastered the art of grandparenting. The Bruins game gave me a chance to redeem myself. Or not.

* * *

I planned every detail of the night, even down to the route I'd take into Boston. I drove east along scenic Storrow Drive so my grandson could see the Charles River on his left and the skyline of Boston rising on his right. As a child I'd regarded my first sight of the city lights as an exciting overture to the game.

As we approach the elegant span of the Longfellow Bridge, I glance in my rearview mirror to see my grandson's reaction. He is sound asleep in his car seat.

Demetre doesn't wake up until I pull into the parking garage and lower my window to take a ticket from the parking attendant, who tells me parking is $25 and, worse, "pay when you leave." The attendant also hands me a sheet of yellow paper with a photocopied message. The message warns of long delays in exiting the garage after the game. "We're going to have to leave the game early or we'll be stuck in this garage for a long time," I say to Demetre. He says nothing and seems not even to have heard me.

I hand our game tickets to a man who scans them with an electronic device and waves us toward an escalator. I bought our tickets at face value from a friend whose season seats are in the front row of the balcony, thus guaranteeing my grandson an unobstructed view.

* * *

More than a half-century earlier I'd sat in what my father's tickets identified as the "Stadium" section of the old Garden, the lower bowl in that steep three-decker arena. My father and I arrived in time for pre-game warm-up. For a few minutes, until my view became partly obscured by men wearing hats and by a haze of cigar smoke, I had a clear view of Detroit's Gordie Howe and Bruins future Hall-of-Famers Leo Boivin and Bill Quackenbush. But it was the goalies, Terry Sawchuk for Detroit and "Sugar Jim" Henry for Boston, who caught and held my eye. The brush-cut, gum-chewing Sawchuk turned aside pucks with cocky efficiency. No move exaggerated. Nothing wasted. Sugar Jim (so nicknamed for a sweet tooth that sometimes had him downing packets or cubes of sugar) moved with a herky-jerky quickness, his face reflecting strain and tension as was understandable in a day when goalies played without helmets or masks. I was struck by what I saw as the glamour of the position. Its action. Its specialized equipment. Its essentialness. In that minute I began to think about becoming a goalie.

* * *

Demetre and I get off the last in a series of escalators and walk along the concourse and toward the stairway leading to our seats. We pass a photo of a Bruins team from the thirties. The photo is unlabeled but it must have been the 1938/'39 Stanley Cup winning team because it shows Eddie Shore and Milt Schmidt and that was the only season they played together on a Cup winner. We walk over to the photo and I point out Shore standing in the back left corner of the picture, the trace of a grin gracing his face. "Your great-great-grandmother saw him play," I say to my grandson, explaining what an important player Shore once was. Demetre doesn't say anything. He is sometimes like a video recorder with only two settings—*play* and *record.* On this night the switch is apparently stuck on *record,* as mine was in similar circumstances so long ago.

We take our seats just as the house lights get brighter. For a moment I think about using the time before warm-up to explain the meaning of all the lines and circles on the ice. Then I think better of it. Let him follow the puck and whatever else interests him. Hockey should be more synthesis than analysis. I can explain things later.

* * *

"You may as well know what you're watching," my father said to me in his gruff and graceless way the afternoon before my first game. He grabbed a pad of yellow lined paper, drew a rink and explained to me the two basic rules, offside and icing. I did not understand either. The only rule I knew was: most goals wins. My understanding of the rules came with my growing interest in the game. In the beginning I watched the puck. And the goalies.

* * *

"If you want something to eat, let's get it now before the teams come out for warm-ups," I say.

"Popcorn," my grandson says.

We walk back along the concourse until we come to a beer stand that also sells popcorn. "Smallest size you have, please," I say to the man at the counter. I may as well have said "Supersize me." The man hands me a cardboard barrel spilling over with heavily salted popcorn. The Bruins and Boston Garden are owned by what is essentially a concession company, Buffalo-based Delaware North, and, as every concessionaire knows, salt moves drinks. "I'd better get a bottle of water," I say to the same man who sold us the popcorn. As he hands me the bottle, he twists off the white plastic cap and throws it in the trash. "Sorry. People have been throwing the caps on the ice," he says.

"Why do they do that?" Demetre asks.

"Maybe because they never played," I say unable to conjure up a better answer. I think people who throw things on the ice and people who boo are the same people. I suspect many of them never set foot in an arena, court or field preferring instead the safety and anonymity of the grandstand. I doubt any of them were goalies. I never heard my father or grandmother boo a player. Once when I was about twelve years old I booed an error-prone Red Sox shortstop named Don Buddin. I did it because some adult fans around me were doing it. But it didn't feel right and I've never done it since.

Kernels of popcorn cascade from the container onto the concourse floor as we walk back to our seats. We pass a poster of Bruins center Patrice Bergeron, a smooth-skating scorer and slick playmaker whom I've come to think of as Jean Ratelle Lite, Ratelle being an ex-Bruins center and Hall of Famer whom I and many others once regarded as Jean Béliveau Lite. "That's Patrice Bergeron my favorite Bruin," I say to my grandson, as I point to the poster.

"Number 37," he says.

We arrive back in our seats just as Bruins goalie Tim Thomas leads the team onto the ice for pre-game. The Ottawa Senators take the ice at the same time and for a few minutes the teams, seen from our seats, look like two churning wheels. "There's number 37," Demetre says, pointing excitedly to Bergeron, who is skating counter clockwise with the insouciant pre-game bounciness that, without fail, makes me wish I were skating instead of sitting.

"They have a lot of pucks," Demetre says, adding, "and they shoot hard."

"They could drive nails with those shots," I say, recycling one of my late father's better lines from what seems a lifetime ago.

The first period is scoreless, something you don't want when you take a kid to his first game. But Demetre seems transfixed by the speed and action. Every few minutes he absentmindedly reaches into the popcorn barrel, but without taking his eyes off the ice. Late in the period my grandson turns his head right to follow the play just as I turn my head left to check out-of-town scores. For a moment I catch sight of his eyes, as round as little faceoff circles.

* * *

We're still nibbling at Mount Popcorn when Ashley Adamson shows up at our seats. On this night Adamson is working as a production assistant for New England Sports Network, which televises most Bruins games. She is a former grad student in a sports journalism course I teach at Boston University. Adamson invites us to visit the new in-stadium studio that NESN has recently opened. She leads us to a private elevator that takes us to the stadium level, then, flashing a pass at a security guard, she ushers us through a door into the studio used for pre- and post-game Bruins shows. She shows Demetre the anchor desk with its built-in TV monitors and introduces him to several people, including analyst, ex-Bruins defenseman and 1982 NHL No. 1 draft pick Gord Kluzak.

Demetre says nothing. "He's on *record* tonight," I explain to Kluzak. "He'll be on *play* tomorrow." Indeed, the next morning when his mother asks him, "What part of the game did you like best?" Demetre says: "The TV studio." I understand this. He is part of the second generation of fans who get most of their sports served up on a beam of electrons. For them the illusion of television becomes the reality of the game. I sometimes think that fans who experience sports only via television become like the people in the parable of the cave:

> *Behold, human beings living in a cave, with its mouth*
> *Open toward the light ... here they have been from their*
> *Childhood ... and can only see the wall of the cave [and]*
> *Shadows which the fire throws on the opposite wall.*
> —Plato, *The Republic*

I am glad to have taken my grandson out of the cave and given him a chance to see the whole ice; to look at what he wants to look at and not at what a director in a truck decides he should look at.

I'd never seen hockey on television or anywhere else except on local skating ponds before I went to my first Bruins game. By the time hockey moved to TV, circa 1960, I knew at first glance that it was a bad marriage. I watch a lot of games on television but, when I do, when anyone does, we have to look at a shot that will be—*must* be—of the action around the puck. In the arena I can look at what I want to look at and that, even today, is the goalies. My father was a goalie. Nothing special. Just club and pond hockey in the days before he enlisted in the army for the Second World War. My father was also a catcher. He used to say goalies and catchers were often the same people, "guys who like to have the play in front of them."

* * *

I forget the goal scorer but I remember the goal: a shot that beat Sawchuk low and clanked against the metal base plate of the old-fashioned, drape-netted Art-Ross-designed goal. After the goal, Sawchuk hopped to his feet, stretched his back and neck, slapped his stick across his pads and got into his crouch to await the center ice face-off. "See that," said my father nudging me with his right elbow and pointing toward Sawchuk. "No emotion. Just chew your gum and never let 'em know how much you're hurt." It would be about a decade before I completely understood that. But when I did, it would be one of the most valuable and enduring lessons of my life.

* * *

Demetre and I return to our seats just as Glen Murray gives Boston a 1–0 lead with a goal at 0:23 of the second period. We both miss it. No problem. We can see it two or three times on the Jumbotron hanging over the middle of the arena. Miss a goal in the fifties and you missed it forever. Today replay will be there to bail you out. We can be sloppy fans.

About four minutes after the first goal, Ottawa's Jason Spezza converts a pass from Dany Heatley to tie the game. My grandson doesn't react. At 13:47 Boston rookie Petr Tenkrat, called up from the American Hockey League's Providence Bruins the day before, lofts a shot past goalie Martin Gerber into the Ottawa net for a 2–1 Boston lead. "I SAW that one," Demetre yells. It's only then that I realize the pace of the game is so fast he'd seen the first two goals only on replay.

I think there is a nostalgic romanticism among those of us who knew the Original Six NHL franchises. We want to think of the game of our era, of our childhood, as being better than today's game. We remember it as a game played by giants, who skated faster and shot harder than today's players. But nostalgia lies. Subtract a Bobby Orr and a Bobby Hull. Deduct a Rocket Richard and maybe a Terry Sawchuk (the most technically proficient of the old stand-up style goalies) and the majority of today's players are faster, stronger, better conditioned and better coached. I look at kinescopes and grainy film from games in the fifties and early sixties, and I know that the hockey I first saw was slower and thus more *fathomable* than what my grandson is trying to comprehend. But what has been gained in athletic excellence has been lost in glamour and romance.

I would be the last person to suggest taking helmets or masks off today's players, be they Pee Wees or pros a puck can kill, and has killed, people. And yet, back in the day of the Original Six, I enjoyed being able to identify players by their face and not their numbers. There was drama in seeing Rangers goalie Gump Worsley grimace as he threw himself in front of yet another shot . . . in Hal Laycoe's eyes, magnified by his glasses, as they darted here and there when he looked for a teammate to pass to . . . in Boom Boom Geoffrion's scowl . . . in Jean Béliveau's blank-faced imperturbability . . . Bobby Hull's cocky wink-and-a-smile menace . . . and Rocket Richard's unrelievedly dark intensity. My grandson will see his NHL stars in tinted visors, players identifiable mainly by block-lettered names above their jersey numbers.

With 3:26 left in the period Murray scores his second goal, giving Boston a 3–1 lead. "YESSS." I say, thrusting my right arm into the air while hugging Demetre with my left. He seems startled. Surprised I care so much. I can recall my father and I leaping to our feet and pounding each other with rolled-up copies of the Boston *Record*, beating the tabloid to shreds when the Bruins scored a go-ahead or winning goal. Now, four decades later, I ask myself a question as my daughter might ask it: Why is it so important to Grandpa Jack?

I think the game itself, that is, the play and the final score, is not so important. But the connection is. The shared experience of the game and the conversations that inevitably follow have been one of the bonds holding my father's family together since the days of the Depression. I recall the obligatory Sunday dinners at my grandmother's house during the fifties and sixties. My grandmother's favorite sport was politics. But when conversation, about the Korean War, the Cold War, the Vietnam War, threatened to become divisive, the Bruins (and Red Sox and Celtics) gave us all a safe conversational harbor. The game wasn't important, the safety was. Hockey was a place to stay until tempers cooled. An argument over whether Bobby Orr was more dominant than Eddie Shore (Orr was) posed a lesser threat than an argument over US military involvement in Southeast Asia. Hockey can drive the poison from the room. It can help hold people together when other things, admittedly more important, pull us apart. That's something worth passing on to another generation. I think my grandmother knew that. She took me to many games but, unlike my father and me, never showed much emotion at a hockey game. I'd been with her at baseball games and horse races where she was vocal and enthusiastic, a ripper of programs and a tearer of pari-mutuel tickets. I know today that her exuberance was probably due to her having a bet on those races and games. (I'm sure she wasn't the first to say it, but Mammam was the first person from whom I heard the line: "Baseball isn't our national pastime. *Betting* on baseball is our national pastime.") Boston bookmakers weren't taking bets on hockey in the fifties and so, in retrospect, I see that my grandmother took me to Bruins games more for my sake than hers. The game wasn't important. Being there was. And that's why I'd brought her great-great-grandson to the Garden on this night.

* * *

A late second-period goal by Ottawa's Chris Neil cuts Boston's lead to 3–2. Worse, Neil's second goal at 1:25 of the third period ties the game, thus creating for me a worst-case scenario, an early exit from a tie game but one that can't possibly end in a tie. Either the Bruins will win or lose in regulation, in a five-minute, four-on-four, sudden-death overtime, or in the dramatic shootout that must follow a scoreless overtime. No matter. I don't like the thought of being stuck in an indoor parking garage breathing exhaust fumes for half an hour while we inch our way toward the collection booths, beyond which will lie a tangle of post-game traffic. I pull the chute.

"Next whistle, Demetre," I say. "We don't want to get stuck in that garage." He nods with Sawchuckian impassivity. I don't know whether he minds or not.

There's a whistle with about eleven minutes left to play in the period. We leave our seats, in the process abandoning a still half-full barrel of popcorn, and scramble up the stairway. I toss the empty capless water bottle into a trash barrel. All the escalators are still running upward, so we find a door marked EXIT and scramble down several long flights of stairs to the street.

We double-time down a ramp toward the parking garage. Dozens of other fans are leaving early, too. My grandson buckles himself into his car seat while I tune into the game on the radio. I hand two tens and a five to a cashier and ease out into the already-building traffic. I whip the car left toward Leverett Circle. Just as we merge onto the speedway that is Storrow Drive westbound, Bruins radio play-by-play announcer Dave Gaucher yells that Patrice Bergeron has scored to give Boston a 4–3 lead with 6:18 to play.

"Yay, Patrice Bergeron," Demetre says from the back seat. He doesn't seem unhappy that he missed seeing the goal.

We listen wordlessly to the rest of the game while I pick my way down Storrow Drive and onto the Massachusetts Turnpike. The Bruins hang on for the win and the radio show is wrapping up with a live-from-the-dressing-room interview with Bergeron when we come to our exit. I pay the toll and sneak a peek into the back seat, where I expect to see my grandson asleep. But he's wide awake, leaning half out of his car seat, staring at the radio as if he expects a picture to suddenly appear. I think briefly of the black plastic Admiral A.M. radio beside which I used to fall asleep listening to Bruins games broadcast by Fred Cusick and sponsored by Carling Black Label Beer. I saw the game in my mind. I knew the name of every Bruins player and most of their opponents. I even knew the words to the "Mabel, Black Label" commercial jingles and to my friends' schoolyard version of same, "Mabel. Mabel. Get off the table. That quarter's for the beer." For every game I attended I heard twenty on radio. I doubt that until our trip home from the Bruins game my grandson had ever heard a game of any kind on a radio.

It's close to 10:30 when I pull into my driveway.

"Well, how was it, Demetre?" Barbara gushes as we come through the front door.

"Good," he says as if showing any enthusiasm might be uncool.

* * *

My father and I had also gotten home at about 10:30, but I had school the next day and was thus immediately sent upstairs to bed. I first went into a spacious upstairs bathroom, wherein, momentarily distracted from the purpose of my visit, I grabbed a rolled-up pair of socks from a laundry basket and began throwing the socks against the bathroom wall and "saving" the ensuing rebounds with a series of spectacular splits and dives, my moves enhanced by the slickness of the linoleum. It is very easy to save a pair of rolled-up socks that are bouncing off a wall. But I wanted none of easy. I wanted crowd-pleasing flamboyance. I wanted sensational. I was Terry Sawchuk and Sugar Jim Henry rolled into one as I dived and sprawled on the linoleum. I'd made seven or eight of these needlessly theatrical saves when my father's voice boomed up the stairwell: "KNOCK IT OFF AND GO TO BED," to which he appended the inevitable: "DON'T MAKE ME COME UP THERE." I went to bed and fell asleep naively hopeful that a great goaltending career had been launched in a second-floor bathroom.

* * *

Demetre puts on his pajamas and brushes his teeth. I am rummaging in the refrigerator when he comes into the kitchen. "Thank you, Grandpa Jack," he says, which is probably what Tracey or Barbara sent him in to say, but he says it sincerely and not as though he were reading it off a TelePrompTer. As soon as he is out of the kitchen I open the liquor cabinet and pour myself a not ungenerous cognac. I'm swirling the cognac in a snifter preparatory to my luxuriating in the first swallow when Tracey comes into the room. She eyes the cognac, then me. "A tough night for Grandpa Jack?" she asks.

"A great night for Grandpa Jack," I say raising my glass to her.

"EXCUSE ME, MR. DELVECCHIO..."

Do what you are afraid to do.
—Mary Moody Emerson
Advice to her nephew Ralph Waldo Emerson

I find it amusing to be in my twentieth year as an adjunct professor at a university from which I once came within a tenth of a percentage point of flunking out and at which I probably still hold the single-season record for disciplinary trips to the assistant dean's office. That record, set in my freshman year of 1963/'64, included one conviction for playing street hockey and breaking a desk in the student government room and another for playing stickball on a newly seeded front lawn. I regard my current job teaching at Boston University's College of Communication the way I regard the former hockey enforcer who drops his gloves and picks up a whistle. Some of those ex-goons are good refs because they know all the tricks and have good rapport with the players, especially the high-penalty-minutes guys. I get along well with my students, most of whom are aspiring sportswriters and all of whom know my only three rules: meet deadlines, play hurt and don't do as I did. From 2000 to 2007 my second-semester sports journalism class met at 8 A.M. on the Monday following the Super Bowl. No student ever missed that class on that day, notwithstanding that the local New England Patriots played in, and won, three of those Super Bowls. I saw some memorable hangovers. But I didn't see empty seats. The kids played hurt.

As for the classroom seats I left empty during my freshman year academic crime spree . . . well, I'd like to say it was the Boston Bruins' fault. But it wasn't. It was my fault for cutting too many psych and bio classes so that I could leave campus early and stop in at the North Station/Boston Garden to watch the end of a Bruins practice, this before I boarded the train for home and my job stocking shelves in a grocery store.

It was my second semester grades in psych and bio that almost made me a full-time member of the grocery department at Converse Supermarket, Winchester, Massachusetts. I worked on the night crew, where I was just average at stocking the soap and canned-goods aisles but where I excelled at turkey bowling, this being a bowling/curling hybrid that involved sliding a frozen turkey down a store aisle into a cluster of soda bottles set up like bowling pins. (The game was made more interesting, not to mention more odiferous, if the pin setter could sneak in a glass bottle of ammonia among the plastic soda containers.)

I was a commuter student for the practical reason that I couldn't afford to live on campus. And I couldn't have afforded even the first semester of my freshman year if I hadn't taken a year off after high school to work and save money and if my father hadn't counted lawn mowing and snow shoveling as services in lieu of rent. Having worked hard to get into college you'd think I'd work hard to *stay* in. Eventually I did. A furious rally in my junior and senior years allowed me to graduate *cum laude*. But my freshman year was a celebration, and abuse, of newfound freedom and an indulgence in spending too much time in my favorite place, Boston Garden, doing my favorite thing, watching some of the best hockey players in the world, who collectively made up one of the worst teams in the NHL.

I recently had occasion to repeat one of those trips from campus to Bruins practice and to remember how being in a rink eased the guilt of a cut class, quieted anything else that might have been troubling me and, on one memorable day more than forty years ago, taught me one of the most important lessons I've ever learned.

* * *

On the morning of Friday September 14, 2007, I was at Boston University editing stories from my sports journalism students when I looked at my watch and saw it was almost 9 A.M. I'd been editing for two hours and had only two or three more stories to go, nothing that couldn't wait until the afternoon. On a whim triggered by nostalgia and the fact that it was a gorgeous late summer day, I decided to walk the two miles from the Boston University campus to the new Boston Garden, officially named the TD Banknorth Garden, where the Bruins were opening training camp at 9:30. When I was a student I often made the trip to the Garden by subway but, on a day as perfect as this one, I would have walked.

Boston is among the most beautiful and walkable of the major American cities. I made it a point to take the same route I used to take as a student. I hustled through Kenmore Square a block south of Fenway Park (another place I occasionally went in lieu of class), walked east along the Commonwealth Avenue mall, past the swan boats not yet hauled out of the pond in the Boston Public Garden, up the broad elm-shaded pathway on the north edge of Boston Common, past the gold-domed State House, down the north slope of Beacon Hill and into the side entrance to the North Station, a railroad station that is attached to the TD Banknorth Garden.

I'm not one of these guys who, if lost, won't ask for directions, but I was embarrassed to have to ask a security guard how to get from the railroad station into the arena. Forty years ago I would have swung around that security guard like Sidney Crosby stickhandling around a rubber cone. Circa 1964 I would have walked into the tunnel leading up from the North Station into the east lobby of the old Garden. Those were days when male college students often wore jackets and ties and carried brief cases. I learned that—clad in this camouflage of respectability and striding purposefully—I would rarely be challenged. Occasionally the half-hearted call of a security guard echoed up the ramp, "Sir? . . . Sir? . . . Excuse me, Sir . . ." But I'd keep walking and the security guard would stop yelling as soon as I rounded the corner of the first section of the ramp. I was stopped at the Garden entrance a few times, but I was never caught from behind. Later I found a way to take an elevator in an adjacent office building up one floor to where a kind of indoor bridge connected the office building to the Garden. That was so easy it made sneaking in almost boring.

Once inside the Garden, I'd walk past the door to the Bruins dressing room and toward the stands to the right of the Zamboni entrance, where I settled into a second- or third-row wooden seat in what was then called the "Promenade" section, the high-rollers' enclave.

I often arrived a few minutes before practice, when the Bruins came clomping out of the dressing room by ones and twos, helmetless and easily identifiable. There was John Bucyk, whom PC revisionist historians claim was nicknamed "Chief" because of his leadership when in reality it was because he looked like the Indian on an old nickel coin. There was tough Teddy Green with the bottom of his jersey tucked into the right corner of his hockey pants . . . perpetually smiling Tom Johnson, a one-time Norris Trophy winner whom the Bruins had acquired in a rare trade with Montreal . . . Tommy Williams, a 1960 Olympic gold medal winner from Duluth . . . Dougie Mohns . . . Murray Oliver . . . Dean Prentice . . . I knew them all.

The players often chatted and joked with each other as they walked toward the ice and while they skated in slow, lazy circles before the formal start of practice. I envied them their happiness, jobs, skill, money, travel, friends, celebrity and short hours.

The Bruins were a terrible team in the early and mid-sixties. In one dismal stretch they finished last four out of five seasons in the then six-team NHL. But I didn't care and neither did the capacity crowds of 13,909 that jammed the old Garden for almost every Bruins home game. We all knew that the losing would end soon. We'd heard reports of the buzz-cut blond teenage defenseman playing for the Oshawa Generals. We believed Bobby Orr would make the Bruins win. We didn't yet know that, in so doing, Orr would also drag hockey out of Canada and the northeast and spread it across a continent.

I went to those pre-Orr *games* to see a bad team play a great sport. I went to *practice* for reasons I think I've only begun to understand. I believe some of my fascination with watching practice had to do with the chance to sprawl in the expensive seats and be close to the players who, in a game, I might be watching from the stadium or balcony seats. And some of the allure had to do with the building. I never spent an unhappy moment in the old Garden. It was as if problems from school or home or work couldn't penetrate those thick, grimy brick walls. I remember thinking several times while watching practice that for thirty or forty minutes no one in the world knew where I was. I liked, and still like, being alone. Sitting by myself in a near-empty Garden was a delightful surcease in my otherwise over-scheduled life. And the fact that it was stolen time, in this case stolen from bio or psych, somehow made it all the sweeter. But it was a sweetness I could not recapture in my most recent foray.

* * *

After asking the security guard for directions into the new Garden I still walked the wrong way and ended up outside of the building looking at the parking lot where the original Garden had stood until 1995. The old Joni Mitchell lyrics rang true—they paved paradise and put up a parking lot. I looked around for the door the security guard had tried to direct me to. I walked back into the building and this time saw another security guard standing near a door leading from the North Station to the main arena. "Right this way, sir. Up the stairs to section 2," he said.

I double-timed it up a flight of stairs onto a concourse where a fan wearing a Bruins hat and a day-old growth of beard wandered around. "Where's section 2?" he asked me.

"I think it's up another flight," I said pointing to an escalator. We rode up together. "They shoulda rebuilt the team before they built a new Gahden," the man said in a heavy Boston accent of the kind that once marked my own speech. The Bruins had finished thirteenth, five places out of the play-offs, in the 2006/'07 season and fan interest in the team was the lowest I'd ever seen. The Red Sox and Patriots dominate the New England sports market. Over the summer of 2007 the Celtics added stars Kevin Garnett and Ray Allen to a roster that already had Paul Pierce, those moves vaulting the Celts over the Bruins in the race for third place in the hearts of New Englanders. For the first time in living memory the Bruins had to *sell* or risk dropping off the New England pro sports radar. The sell began as soon as I walked into section 2.

There were only fourteen fans watching practice when I arrived, this notwithstanding numerous newspaper and web-site announcements that practice was open to the public. (I think entering the building legitimately, as opposed to sneaking in, took a lot of the fun out of it for me.) An eight-by-ten sheet of paper taped to each chair in section 2 offered season ticket packages for sale in full-season, half-season, ten-game or six-game packs. As recently as the nineties all the Bruins had to do to sell tickets was to announce the schedule.

I looked down at the ice and recognized only two skaters, captain Zdeno Chara and new coach Claude Julien. The others were just helmeted and often visored troglodytes whirling around in the complicated flow drills that have become so popular since the 1980s and the ascent of the Wayne Gretzky–led Edmonton dynasty. I thought that watching a modern practice wasn't exactly like seeing a late-1960s scrimmage with Bobby Orr on one team, Phil Esposito on the other and Gerry Cheevers in goal. I wondered if the Bruins, and the so-called new NHL, were becoming irrelevant even to me, a hockey lifer.

Section 2 was cordoned off by bright yellow tape of the kind police use to mark crime sites. Thus I couldn't walk over to an adjacent section where some writer friends, including one of my former students, gathered in a media-only area. Nor was there any direct access to the players, who no longer have to walk through the stands—and fans—en route to the ice, but who now walk from the dressing room to a door behind the team bench and this on a floor of the building inaccessible to fans. I had no sense of proximity even when the players were on the ice. The protective glass running along the sides of the rink is now so high that you have to be sitting ten or twelve rows back just to see over it. That glass used to be so low that linesmen and refs routinely grabbed the top of it to hoist themselves out of harm's way.

I recalled a day shortly after Johnny "Pie" McKenzie was traded from New York to Boston. The Bruins were finishing practice with a simple skating drill in which half the players skated the width of the rink and back. While McKenzie waited for his group to go, he reached up over the glass and shook hands with a smattering of fans as if he were a candidate running for office. "Hi, I'm John McKenzie. . . . Hi, I'm John McKenzie. . . ." I could hear him from where I stood. Today a player couldn't reach over the glass even if he wanted to. And I wonder if any would want to.

Thomas Wolfe was right. You can't go home again. There was none of the old magic that morning. No feeling of having stolen the time, no real interest in the players on the ice, no fascination with the sterile new building whose walls were not thick enough to keep out thoughts of pending writing deadlines, household chores and a to-do list growing unmanageably long. I was antsy and bored. Whatever I'd hoped to find in the new Garden wasn't there anymore. I was alone in a large building and on my own time. My mind wandered and, maybe because it was a Friday, my thoughts drifted back to another Friday in the 1963/'64 season.

I'd blown off yet another psych class and had ducked into the old Garden on my way home. But the Bruins weren't on the ice. Boston had apparently practiced early and the Detroit Red Wings were waiting to use the ice. Maybe they'd played a Thursday-night game and were practicing at the Garden before moving on to their next stop. Or maybe they'd come in early for a Saturday game. I don't recall. But I was grateful for the chance to see a different team practice. A few Detroit players sat in the "Promenade" seats waiting for the Zamboni to finish resurfacing the ice. This was the great Red Wings team of Gordie Howe, Norm Ullman, Alex Delvecchio and legendary goaltender Terry Sawchuk in his last season with Detroit before he was traded to Toronto. The vision that stays with me is of Delvecchio in full practice uniform, his gloves on the seat beside him, casually smoking a cigar while waiting to take the ice. I looked around for Sawchuk but didn't see him. Then, as now, I considered Sawchuk to be the most technically perfect of the old-fashioned stand-up goaltenders. I wanted to watch him work. I climbed into the Promenade section and stood about twenty feet to Delvecchio's right, where a draft from the open Zamboni entrance doors carried the cigar smoke toward me. I kept eying the doorway that led from the dressing rooms to the arena hoping I'd see Sawchuk emerge. Other players came out and waited but there was no sign of Sawchuk. Or of any goalie. It was the absence of a goaltender and the proximity of practice that drove me to consider an impulsive and ill-thought-out act. I would offer my services to the Detroit Red Wings as a practice goaltender. Why not? I'd played goal on a pretty good Catholic Youth Organization team and still played weekends on a club team. If the Wings had the equipment, I had the time.

And the inclination. I wanted the experience and what I fancied would be the story of a lifetime. But first I had to get over the fear. Not the fear of being hurt and humiliated, those were givens, but the fear of asking.

I've always been shy. If I'd gone to more psych classes maybe I'd know why. But why doesn't matter. The blunt reality is that in any social situation I'm struck by a straitening paralysis of anxiety. I don't stay long at parties, I'm reluctant to use the telephone, I don't like talking to anyone I don't know, and my stage fright before lectures is stomach-turning even though I've been teaching since 1987. Such is my anxiety over lecturing that the alarm clock I set for 5 A.M. has gone off exactly *once* in the last seven years. Anxiety awakens me before 4 A.M. on the days I teach. By 7:45, fifteen minutes before my first class, I'm either walking off the butterflies or sitting hunched over at my desk summoning the will to walk through the classroom door. What I feel is exactly what I felt before hockey games as a youth, an overwhelming sense of responsibility and a fear that I may not be equal to it. But I have a consoling theory about this: I believe fear can feed performance. Most of us know from playing that it's the game we're *not* nervous about in which we're likely to play badly. I also know something I used to hear Barbara tell our son and daughter, "the only way out is through." Stage fright, like pre-game anxiety, goes away with the first action. The first save. Or the first hit. Five minutes into most lectures I'm confident, in full oratorical flight and, if the anonymous post-semester student evaluations are to be believed, informative and entertaining. But the hours before that lecture are hellish and will remain so for as long as I teach. I simply don't want to walk into that classroom any more than I wanted to walk up to a veteran NHL player and ask if he needed a practice goalie. But I did want to play and this time the only way *in* was through.

I had to act fast. The Zamboni was on its last lap; more Detroit players had emerged from the dressing room (although there was still no goalie) and Delvecchio was looking around for a place to ditch his cigar. I suppose I targeted Delvecchio because he was sitting nearest to me, but also, I think, because he was an alternate captain and one of the league's true gentlemen, or so I'd read. I forced my way through the fear. I wasn't taking notes, so I can't tell you, verbatim, what I said. But I can tell you what my first four words were, "Excuse me, Mr. Delvecchio . . . " I said coming up on his right, which was his blind side because he was turned slightly toward the Zamboni doors on the left. He didn't turn around at first and for a second I thought he wasn't going to respond at all. I was ready to speak louder when he slowly stood up and turned toward me, a scrawny kid wearing what was then my standard school uniform, blue blazer, blue button-down shirt, rep tie, chinos, penny loafers. I hoped I looked sincere. I can't tell you the exact sequence of words that followed but, as best I remember it, I said, "If you need a practice goalie I played some in school and I'd be glad to stand in if you have the equipment."

Delvecchio didn't laugh at me. He didn't answer me either. Not right away. Instead he turned and looked at the gaggle of players waiting near the Zamboni doors. Sure enough, no goalie.

Could I have pulled off the greatest coup of my life? Was I about to trade Psych 101 for a chance to face Gordie Howe in a for-real NHL practice? And what if I played well? My mind was soaring, reeling with possibility, when Delvecchio asked a teammate, a player I didn't recognize, "Hey, we got a goalie today?"

My God, Delvecchio sounded interested in my offer. This was heady stuff. I was one "Nah, we need someone" away from the show. It was as close as I ever got.

"Yeah," the player said to Delvecchio and then said a name I didn't recognize save to say it wasn't Terry Sawchuk. "He'll be out in a minute," the player said. Delvecchio turned back to me. "Thanks, son," he said, "but we've got someone."

I tried not to look as crushed as I felt. Never let 'em know how much you're hurt is an old rule of goaltending and of life. I walked back to where I'd been standing. The Zamboni clanked off the ice, the players went on and, sure enough, a goaltender who was not Terry Sawchuk came waddling up the ramp toward the ice. I stayed and watched a few minutes of practice (Jeez, I could have played in the *other* net) before I slunk out to the Boston & Maine train that would carry me to my job in the grocery store, which seemed at that moment to be as far from the show as one could get.

Until now I've never written about that day at the Red Wings' practice and I've rarely talked about it. I didn't want to sound like the fisherman talking about the one that got away. And I never spent much time thinking about it until that recent Friday, forty-three seasons after the fact, that I walked from the Garden back to Boston University. I recalled the feelings: the anxiety, the sudden soaring hope, the even more sudden disappointment. And I began to think that maybe the fish didn't get away. I decided that if approaching Delvecchio wasn't a smart thing to do, it was at least a good thing to have tried. I went through the wall of fear and shyness. The moment I said "Excuse me, Mr. Delvecchio . . . " I had paid the price and pushed myself out of the comfort zone. Asking was more important—and, for me, harder—than playing would have been. You don't learn that in psych class, you only learn *about* it. The biggest lessons are learned out of the classroom where life is the teacher or, perhaps more accurately, where we teach ourselves. Pushing through the wall of fear didn't make the fear go away. It didn't make me less shy. But it proved to me that I could go through the wall when I wanted to. I may be scared but I'm not unwilling.

I didn't stop going to Bruins practices during my college years, but I did learn that classes and practice were not mutually exclusive. Following my near-disastrous freshman year, I went to class when I was supposed to and to Bruins practice when I could. First I became dependable. Then I got good grades. And by doing those things in that order, I learned another lesson I try to teach my students: dependability beats talent if talent isn't dependable. I haven't yet told them how I learned that. Or where. But I will. That's what teachers do. I am the goon turned ref.

BACK TO THE BARNS

They are all gone,
And I alone sit lingering here;
Their very memory is fair and bright,
And my sad thoughts doth clear.
—Henry Vaughan, "They Are All Gone"

Visiting the site of our team's old stadium is like driving past the home of our first teenage crush—bittersweet and vaguely unsettling. Why does it matter? Why do we still care?

It matters because there was a time when what happened in that building was important to us. The arenas were places we went with the people who mattered: fathers, mothers, sisters, brothers, grandparents, teammates, dates and friends. If you're one of the shrinking, and today irreplaceable, group who once saw an NHL game in Boston Garden, Chicago Stadium, Detroit's Olympia Stadium, Toronto's Maple Leaf Gardens, the Montreal Forum or New York's Madison Square Garden (the old one on 50th Street and 8th Avenue, not the current one at Pennsylvania Plaza), then you know what I'm talking about. These are places where generations of us sat together, cheered together, fell in love with our sport and, though few of us saw it coming, became infatuated with a building and the memories it held. Those old arenas, the four in the United States demolished, the two in Canada radically changed and no longer hosting NHL games, instilled in some of us a reverence that we retain and that, in many cases, we try to pass on to those who were never there and now, sadly, never can be.

I saw NHL games in four of the so-called Original Six arenas, Boston, Chicago, Montreal and Toronto, and had a pilgrim's look at the buildings in New York and Detroit. Here is a fanning of old flames that for many of us will never stop flickering.

Boston Garden

The Boston Garden was the most important building in my life after my home and school. My father and I started going to Bruins games at the Garden in the 1954/'55 NHL season, the same time that my mother was stricken with terminal cancer. A trip to a Sunday-night game was sometimes the epilogue to an afternoon at the hospital. I think that the game, and the enchantingly grubby interior of the Garden itself, offered a brief release from the unknowableness of childhood in general and of that dark winter in particular. I was never unhappy in the Garden because my thoughts could never range beyond its walls.

Seen from the outside, the Garden, which my father, like millions of Bostonians, pronounced *Gah-den*, was a squat brick box, its long windows painted dark blue. It sat surrounded by a hotel on its west side, an elevated Metropolitan Transit Authority railway to the south, the Boston & Maine railroad yards to the north and a dark alley, Accolon Way, to the northeast. The entrance to a second balcony, the cheap seats, was on Accolon Way. In my teenage years my friends and I would sometimes sneak into Bruins games via the alley. There was only one usher, sometimes backed up by a police officer, on duty at that gate. If the cop wasn't there or was momentarily distracted—"Move that cah. Ya cahn't pahk here."—it was an easy matter to scoot past the usher and up the long stairwell to the second balcony, where we would get lost in the crowd. The usher could have chased us but never did. We weren't worth a coronary.

The main entrances to the other sections, the stadium and first balcony, were drab cement ramps leading in from the sidewalk along Causeway Street. My father and I always took the first of the two ramps at the top turn of which a man who was a double amputee sat on a folded blanket and held a cup of freshly sharpened pencils. My father would plunk a coin in the cup and take a pencil. "There's always someone worse off than you are," he'd say.

We smelled the Garden before we saw it. Near the top of the ramp leading into the east lobby we'd be hit by a cool current of air wafting in from the ice surface and carrying with it the mingled smells of popcorn, pizza, smoke and beer. We followed it like salmon heading upstream.

At first we bought our tickets at the lobby box office, taking our chances as to where we'd sit. But with the mid-sixties rumors of the coming of *Wunderkind* Bobby Orr, my father stretched our modest family budget and bought season tickets. Having been a goalie, he bought them behind the net. Section G. Row E. Seats 3 and 4. Hard wooden seats five rows behind the goal judge and just about even with the top of the protective glass that was much lower in those days. You paid attention during pre-game warm-ups because, if you didn't, sooner or later you'd have your hair parted by a shot or deflection. These were great seats to have during a time that would come to be called the "Golden Age of Goalies." For much of the sixties, I crouched in my seat just a few feet away from the likes of Detroit's Terry Sawchuk, Chicago's Glenn Hall, Montreal's Jacques Plante, New York's Gump Worsley, Toronto's John Bower, Hall of Famers all, and a succession of long-suffering Bruins goalies, with Eddie Johnston being the best of this abused lot.

It was from those seats that I first saw Bobby Orr, the only player who could dominate a game in all three zones. "He couldn't be as good as Eddie Shore," my grandmother said until my father took her to a game. "I've never seen anyone like him," came my grandmother's amended opinion. No one has.

I was in the Garden for the building's most dramatic moment when on, May 10, 1970, Orr, in his fourth season, clinched the Stanley Cup in overtime of Game 4 by whipping a Derek Sanderson pass behind St. Louis goalie Glenn Hall for a 4–3 Bruins win. Orr then took his famous celebratory dive, enhanced by Blues' defenseman Noel Picard's trip, frozen forever by the lens of photographer Ray Lussier. There was the ultimate player in his ultimate moment on one of hockey's great stages. The cheers of the Gallery Gods, the denizens of the second balcony colloquially known as "the Heaven," and of all of us rained down on Orr and the jubilant Bruins. The building shook.

For decades there was talk of refurbishing or replacing the Garden, but, until the opening of a new arena in 1996, all that talk produced was a digital scoreboard, a few luxury boxes up where the Gallery Gods used to sit (odd that the cheapest seats were replaced by the most expensive) and a coat of yellow paint that was supposed to brighten the interior but was so flat and washed out that it only made the place look dingier. The old Garden was no "lyric bandbox," as John Updike would accurately describe Boston's other landmark stadium, Fenway Park. I didn't care. I loved the joint.

The Garden's successor—The TD Banknorth Garden—has wide concourses, capacious restrooms and dozens of concession stands. It has luxury suites, private clubs and premium seating at various price levels. It is an antiseptically bright and coldly tidy place in which to watch a game. I think most of the younger fans think the new building is a big improvement over the old brick barn. Soon there will be an entire generation who never set foot in the original Garden. As my father said, there are always people worse off than you.

Montreal Forum

The building I still regard as the most important in hockey history always unsettled me. I never entered the place without feeling like a trucker who'd pulled off the road for lunch and inadvertently wandered into a five-star French restaurant. The

Forum intimidated and impressed the same way an exclusive restaurant intimidates and impresses, with protocol, tradition and language. I responded to my discombobulation in odd and mostly ineffective ways.

When I worked full-time as a sportswriter, I made it a point to wear a jacket and tie to every NHL game I covered. But I took it up a sartorial notch for assignments in Montreal, where I wore the jacket and tie to *practice*, a *suit* to games. When I was in the "Cathedral of Hockey," I wanted to at least look like I belonged. Feeling like I belonged was another and more elusive matter.

The distraction began when, walking west on St. Catherine or De Maisonneuve, I'd first catch sight of the building, not that the exterior of the Forum had much to recommend it. Indeed, the brick-and-steel structure was, on the outside, the least attractive of the Original Six arenas. The Forum was built in 129 days in 1924 and remodeled twice. Its most interesting exterior feature was two escalators which, when illuminated at night and seen from the sidewalk, looked like giant crossed hockey sticks. It was on the inside that the Forum overwhelmed you.

It started with the ghosts. The Canadiens won twenty-two of their record twenty-four Stanley Cups as residents of the Forum and those flags, hanging like laundry from the ceiling, never let me forget that the Forum was to hockey rinks what St. Peter's is to basilicas. In my native Boston, no doubt because the Bruins suffered so many losses at the Forum, we talked about the building's ghosts as if the phantom sticks of Howie Morenz and Aurèle Joliat were sweeping pucks toward the visitor's net while the ghostly limbs of Georges Vezina and Jacques Plante were stopping Bruins shots.

More tangible if no less intimidating than the ghosts was the Canadiens' living royal lineage. In the 1980s when I covered games at the Forum for a US magazine, there existed an unbroken line of French-Canadian superstars stretching back to the 1940s, many of whom I saw in the media room, at practice or in the dressing room. I saw silver-haired Maurice Richard, weighty, quiet, seemingly humorless, burdened with his decades of having been a symbol of and for the French Canadian people . . . the elegant and vaguely ungraspable Jean Béliveau, hockey's Cary Grant and the Canadiens' de facto ambassador, three-quarters of an inch of white cuff extending below a gorgeously tailored suit . . . Henri Richard, quiet and intense but without his brother's gravitas . . . Jacques Plante, as haughty and aloof as a sommelier, a man sure of his wine list, his dinner and himself . . . Guy Lafleur, a man seemingly as ill at ease and self-conscious off the ice as he was smooth and secure on it. I saw them all but, save for one brief interview with Lafleur and with Plante, I never presumed to speak to them. You let gods speak first.

I entered the building through the press gate on Atwater Avenue and went directly to the media room, where the walls fairly dripped with framed color photographs of former Canadiens' captains. The mystique was everywhere. Though all signs and media game notes were in English and French, I never truly felt the language difference until the late Claude Mouton's voice boomed over the public address system: "ACCUEILLONS . . . LET'S WELCOME . . . NOS CANADIENS . . ." And the cheers would begin and grow louder mounting in volume long after the cheers in other arenas would have stopped and you could hear and feel and see that this place was somehow different. Hockey meant more here.

Maybe because I was always emotionally supercharged on game day at the Forum, or maybe because of my mother's family's roots in French Canada, or maybe just because it's a beautiful song, I always felt deeply moved when the late tenor Roger Doucet, whom I never saw wearing anything but a tuxedo, thrust out his chest and sang the best rendition of an anthem I've heard in any arena in any sport in any country ever:

O Canada
Terre de nos aïeux
Ton front est saint
De fleurons glorieux

The little distinctions were everywhere. In the Forum's executive dining room, which had its own label, *Château du Forum*, on the house wine. In the dress of the patrons, especially in those New Year's Eve games, where I often saw men in tuxedos and women draped in gowns and expensive coats.

Style is more than superficial adornment. It extends to manners and is an easy, graceful way of doing things. I once briefly lost my then ten-year-old daughter Tracey in the Forum. I'd taken her to Montreal for the 1983 Entry Draft and for some sight-seeing. The draft was a one-day affair then. Tracey and I somehow got separated during the lunch break. I was on the edge of panic when I ran into the dapper septuagenarian

Camil DesRoches, once Canadiens PR director and then a sort
of ambassador without portfolio, and told him I was desper-
ately looking for my daughter. Blonde hair. Blue dress. He said
he would help me look.

A few months ago, Tracey, now married and with two children whom she hardly ever loses, recalled that, on seeing her
wandering around in the Forum, DesRoches introduced himself, told her I was looking for her, and invited her to lunch in
the Canadiens' private dining room. He said he would have me
paged. "I wasn't lost," Tracey insists to this day.

I don't recall hearing a page, but when, in my frenetic search,
I stuck my head in the dining room, I was relieved to see Tracey
and Monsieur DesRoches having lunch. I joined them. When
Tracey and I got up to leave, DesRoches stood, bowed slightly
and kissed my daughter's hand. Trace smiled graciously. Then,
as we left the room, she whispered to me: "His mustache tick-
led."

When I think of most of the old arenas, I think of having
been there for a special game or historical moment. But my
lingering memory of the Forum is of once having played there.
In April of 1987 I played in a media game. It surprised me that
as I walked out of the visitors' dressing room and took my first
stride onto hockey's most storied ice my only thought was, try
not to fall.

I took my wife, Barbara, to a game at the Forum in 1996,
about two weeks before they shut the place down. At dinner after the game, I told Barb that, unlike the other five arenas of the
Original Six, I viewed the Forum less as a childhood crush and

more as an impossibly sophisticated, amorous and unreachable icon. I threw out three names, all dated, Katharine Hepburn, Jacqueline Kennedy, Grace Kelly. But I wanted a more contemporary reference, so I asked Barb who, among current celebrities, would carry that degree of intimidating duende.

She thought for a moment and said: "There's no one like that anymore."

Chicago Stadium

This is the best stadium I ever heard. The place seemed built for noise. None of the building's outer walls were more than one hundred feet from the ice and fans seemed to be stacked atop each other in two almost frighteningly steep balconies. Blackhawks crowds began cheering during "The Star-Spangled Banner" at "The rockets' red glare" for regular season games, but sometimes getting out of the gate at "O say, can you see" for a playoff, and standing-room crowds approaching twenty thousand would be in full-throated roar before the puck dropped. But that was mere overture.

It didn't take too many trips to the Chicago Stadium before I learned to cover my ears when the Blackhawks scored, because it was then that organist Al Melgard unleashed the most unforgettable sound in hockey history. The stadium's 25-keyboard, 883-stop, 40,000-pipe Barton organ was a musical battleship. Melgard could press a couple of keys and produce a sound so loud it hurt your ears. The Blackhawks' media guide claimed that the organ could produce a volume equal to that of twenty-five brass bands. To me it sounded more like twenty-five Van Halens with the volume dial set on "10" and my head stuck in a speaker. If played at full volume, which it apparently never was, the organ would reportedly have broken every pane of glass in the building.

I saw about a dozen games in the stadium, all of them from a press box curiously located behind one of the goals and close enough to the ice to make journalists aware of hockey's oldest rule: keep your head up. I had trouble concentrating on my stories in the stadium press box, first because I was afraid of getting hit by a puck and second because I could never stop Sinatra's "Chicago" from playing on the jukebox of my mind.

The dressing rooms at Chicago Stadium were below ice level, so that when players left the ice via a small door behind the net, they had to walk awkwardly down a stairwell, like sweating troglodytes descending to some mysterious cave. Even today when I come in off of my backyard rink and go down the bulkhead stairs into my cellar, I can't help but think of Chicago Stadium.

I arrived in Chicago too late to see the great teams of Bobby Hull, Stan Mikita, Glenn Hall and Elmer "Moose" Vasko. But from what I saw of them on TV and from what I later learned of the city, those teams were perfect for Chicago, playing as they had with a boisterous hard-hitting style that made a Blackhawks game seem like the spillover of a Saturday night on Rush Street.

By the time I got to ChiTown the hockey show was all about Denis Savard's magical spin-o-ramas and goalie Tony Esposito's butterflying saves. Yet the night I would most like to have been in the building has more to do with Chicago's fans than with its players and is, I think, one of the most significant, noble and overlooked moments in NHL history. Today it is accepted hockey protocol that the team clinching the Stanley Cup will parade it around the arena. But this was not always so. For many years the winning team's captain would merely lift the Cup in a kind of photo op. But on the night of May 18, 1971, in Chicago Stadium and in the immediate aftermath of Montreal's 3–2 Cup-clinching win over the Blackhawks, Canadiens captain Jean Béliveau, who had just played his final game, lifted the Cup and began skating around the stadium with the trophy held aloft. The significance of the moment and of the fans' reaction was best described by *The New Yorker* magazine's legendary writer Herbert Warren Wind, who was in the building and who at once grasped the meaning of the moment:

> *The Blackhawk fans, despite their disappointment at the*
> *loss, perceived almost instantly that they were looking*
> *at no conquering foe but at a rare gentleman whose manner*
> *as he displayed the Cup unmistakeably said, "I am not*
> *merely celebrating the Canadiens' triumph, I am celebrating*
> *the superb game of ice hockey and what it means to all of us...."*
> *Since that time the circling of the rink with the huge trophy*
> *held aloft has come to be regarded as the perfect ending to*
> *the perfect season.*

In cheering Béliveau the most boisterous crowd in the most boisterous building provided the game with a moment of nobility and a tradition of grace that should make us all proud to be hockey fans.

Madison Square Garden

I'm told my paternal grandmother came into the world in the usual way, though it seems to me she might well have been sent by Damon Runyon. She was one of those Guys and Dolls–Era types whose many enduring contributions to my education included teaching me how to read the charts in the *Daily Racing Form*. I was in fifth grade at the time.

When, in April of 1960, my grandmother decided I should see Manhattan (the Bronx and Staten Island too), nothing would do but that we would stay in a suite at the then swank Hotel Astor and that an all-day tour of the city would be via Checker cab. My grandmother liked mass transit about as much as she liked horses in outside post positions. She hired a native New York cabbie (think Al Pacino in a scally cap) to show us the good, the bad and the ugly of the city she considered the greatest in the world and the epicenter of the known universe.

After going from Harlem to the Battery and from Park Avenue to the Bowery, the cabbie drove back toward the Astor. But he couldn't pull up close to the hotel because it was cordoned off by police. "It's for Castro," a cop explained. That was the week that Fidel Castro, whose rebel army had four months earlier deposed Cuban dictator Fulgencio Batista, visited New York to give a speech to the United Nations. Castro must have had a meeting or a visit at the Astor. We knew he wasn't staying there because he and his entourage had made a big deal out of disdaining downtown hotels for a hotel in Harlem. "I can let yuz off here or we can go see something else," the cabbie said to my grandmother.

"Is there anything else you want to see?" my grandmother asked me.

"Can we see where the Rangers play?" I asked.

"Madison Square Garden, 50th and 8th, please," my grandmother said to the driver, who was only too happy to drive there, Mr. Pacino knowing a Hall of Fame fare when he had one.

It impressed me that my grandmother knew the street address. It shouldn't have. While my grandmother wagered legally on horse racing, she also bet on baseball and boxing via illegal bookmakers. Many of those boxing matches were at Madison Square Garden. Thus the Garden became a place my grandmother visited to exercise an enthusiastic vigilance over her investments.

There was no hockey at the Garden that day. The final round of the Stanley Cup play-offs (yes, they used to end in April, really, honest) was being played between Montreal and Toronto. I said something about it being too bad that the Rangers, terrible in those days, weren't in the play-offs because, if they were, we could have seen a game. My grandmother said something to the effect that she wouldn't bet on the Rangers even if the game were over. My grandmother said a lot of things it took me years to understand.

The exterior of the Garden was a disappointment. It was just a squat, blocky building with a little portico-like extension hanging over the sidewalk. I stared at it wishing I'd been inside the building six months earlier for an event that was important to me because it involved my favorite player, Montreal goalie Jacques Plante, and is important to me now because I know it was a defining moment in the evolution of hockey.

Six minutes into the first period of a November 1, 1959, game, Rangers forward Andy Bathgate shot a backhander that ripped into Plante's face, opening cuts on his cheek and nose. After getting stitched up, Plante made it a condition of his return to the net that he be allowed to wear a face mask he'd been using in practice. I would like to have heard the murmur of surprise rippling through the Garden when Plante skated out to the Canadiens' net wearing that ghoulish, form-fitting mask (the first seen in the NHL since Clint Benedict's brief experiment with a mask in 1929). Plante backstopped Montreal to a 3–1 win. From that moment on goaltending, indeed hockey itself, would never be the same. Plante's mask not only made goaltending safer but it changed the very architecture of the position, allowing goalies to crouch lower, thus opening the way for what would become the butterfly style of goaltending. Anyone who ever plays goal owes something to Jacques Plante.

Ever since I'd boarded the American Airlines DC-6 for our trip to New York, I'd been taking snapshots with a Brownie Instamatic camera. I'd shot everything from the Empire State Building to a picture of a man in Harlem who had the ace of spades on the upper left side of his jersey and who told me he was, "the hobo king of the underworld." I still have the photo. But I don't have a photo of Madison Square Garden because at the moment I went to shoot it I was out of film. Small matter, because what I truly wanted to see was the interior of the building. I'd seen it in photographs. It looked much like Boston Garden because the two buildings were built and owned by the same company, Madison Square Garden Corp. And yet in a way I had seen the inside of the Garden five years earlier when, in the then new magazine *Sports Illustrated,* I read William Faulkner's description of the first hockey game he'd ever seen, the Rangers vs. the Canadiens at Madison Square Garden. The story ran on page 15 of the January 24, 1955, issue. At the time I didn't know who Faulkner was (what does a kid know about Nobel laureates?), but I knew in some intuitive way that his description was special and different and didn't simply tell me about the building but grabbed me by the hand and pulled me inside, to wit:

> *. . . concentric tiers rising in sections stipulated by the hand lettered names of individual fan club idols, vanishing upward into the pall of tobacco smoke trapped by the roof, the roof which stopped and trapped all that intent and tense watching and concentrated it downward upon the glare of ice frantic and frenetic with motion.*

To paraphrase something Faulkner would say later, there are times when a pen, like a memory, is a more complete instrument of expression than a camera.

Maple Leaf Gardens

It took me a few seasons to realize that, in Toronto, the word was "Gardens" with an *s* while in Boston it was "Garden" singular. The word, as used in North America to describe a public gathering place, goes back to the nineteenth century when "Garden" or "Gardens" was a popular euphemism for "theater," a word that in those days smacked of vice in general and booze in particular. "Garden" or "Gardens" sounded better.

My work as a sportswriter took me to Maple Leaf Gardens about thirty times, with all but one of those visits coming after 1982. But my first look at Maple Leaf Gardens came via photos in the cheesy hockey magazines of the 1950s and '60s. That's where I first saw the rink's most distinguishing feature, a huge portrait of Canada's sovereign, the Queen. The Queen gazed out of her maroon-draped frame like an all-seeing chaperone. If my hometown rink, Boston Garden, was a kind of rollicking blue-collar neighborhood bar, Toronto's Maple Leaf Gardens struck me as being more like a church or museum, cleaner, quieter and filled with people whose blood was bluer than their collars. A lot of men wore overcoats, jackets and ties. Indeed, until 1964, male season ticket holders in the expensive lower seats were *required* to wear jackets and ties.

Photos showed rows of seats sweeping upward in color-coded sections of blue, red, green and gray. None of the 14,850 seats had an obstructed view. (There were 588 obstructed view seats in Boston Garden and I think I sat in each of them.) When I finally entered the Gardens for the first time in the late sixties, the Queen's portrait was gone, removed to make way for more seats, but that other Gardens landmark, radio announcer Foster Hewitt's famed "gondola," still hung from the lip of the press box and did indeed look like the gondola of a blimp.

I was struck by the restraint of a Gardens crowd. Aside from Toronto goals, which were cheered lustily, much of the applause was of the polite opera house variety: correct, reserved and no longer or louder than necessary. If a trip to one of the other five NHL rinks was an invitation to a raucous teenage party at a friend's house while his parents were away, a trip to Maple Leaf Gardens was a date with a debutante to a prep school cotillion. All white gloves and propriety. Enjoy the dance but behave yourself.

When, as a sportswriter, I visited the Gardens, I spent a disproportionate amount of time looking at the old photographs lining the walls, especially the ones from the 1960s, so many of them showing Bobby Baun, Carl Brewer, Frank Mahovlich and Allan Stanley. Next to his beloved Bruins, these had been my father's favorite teams. He liked their clutch-and-grab defense and the wily toughness with which they played. I preferred the bravura of the Canadiens. The arguments were endless. My father would have loved seeing those old photographs. And I would have loved showing them to him. But by then it was too late.

The moment that I wish I'd been in the Gardens took place on April 21, 1951, and the photo of it, credited to the Turofsky Brothers Studio, is nearly as famous and dramatic as the 1970 photo of Bobby Orr flying through the air after scoring the Cup winner. The photo taken at the Gardens shows Toronto's Bill

Barilko crashing to the ice as his high backhander goes sailing past Montreal goalie Gerry McNeil at 2:53 of overtime of Game 5 of the Stanley Cup finals. That goal won the Cup for Toronto. I think the white gloves came off that night.

That was the last goal Barilko, then twenty-four, would score. He died that summer in the crash of a private float plane while on a fishing trip to the Seal River north of Timmins, Ontario. The Leafs would not win another Cup until 1962, the year the wreckage of that plane and the skeletons of Barilko and his fishing buddy and friend, Henry Hudson, were finally recovered.

Maple Leaf Gardens closed in 1999 when the Leafs relocated to the new 18,819-seat Air Canada Centre on fashionable Bay Street. I've been there twice. It seems like most new arenas, clean, functional, bright and sterile.

* * *

It was a few minutes before 5 A.M. on a Friday in early January 2007 when I awoke in my room in Toronto's Royal York Hotel. I was in the city on business but, with nothing to do until 10 A.M., I decided to walk to the old Gardens. I went north on an increasingly seedy Yonge Street and turned right onto Carlton. There was the huge old building, its portico still reading "Maple Leaf Gardens" but its fifteen glass doors closed and papered over. Eight of the seventeen lights under the portico were broken. The nine that worked cast a spooky glow onto the pavement. The last time I'd been here was for a Toronto vs. Dallas Stars game and the sidewalks had been alive with arriving fans and with at least a half-dozen men asking "Need tickets?"

But on this dark morning one large man stood across the street in front of the twenty-four-hour Golden Griddle Family Restaurant. I was taking notes but, at the top of my field of vision, I saw the man move slowly toward me. He made me uneasy. I kept writing, pretending not to notice. But when the man was halfway across Carlton Street I pocketed my notebook and walked past him to the place he had just left. From the sidewalk in front of the restaurant, I saw seven long dark windows on the front of the building and, above those, three flagpoles each with a Maple Leafs flag blowing east in a rising wind. A billboard on the southeast corner of the building read: A LANDMARK FOR 75 YEARS. MAPLE LEAF GARDENS. I was writing this in my notebook when the man who'd crossed the street came back toward me again. The man had me worried. I slipped into the Golden Griddle and sat down at a table. The man glanced briefly into the restaurant then continued walking west toward Yonge Street. An elderly waitress, a career waitress, I thought, came to take my order. She was about to walk away when I asked her: "What's going to happen to Maple Leaf Gardens?"

"They're going to make a Loblaws out of it," she said.

"You mean the grocery store chain?" I said.

"They're working on it now," she said turning and heading for the kitchen. But she went only a few feet before she looked back and said. "Isn't that AWFUL," then continued on her way, not waiting for me to answer.

Olympia Stadium

My first look at the arena everyone called, and I still call, "the Detroit Olympia" (its proper name was Olympia Stadium), came via an Associated Press wire photo that I've kept for fifty years. I recently found my old scrapbook and, in it, that photo barely held in place by yellowing cellophane tape and scissored so close that it doesn't have the name of the Boston paper it ran in but still carries my notation "1956." The picture shows the Red Wings' grimacing Alex Delvecchio with a headlock on the Bruins' Hal Laycoe, whose noggin Delvecchio is ramming into the chain-link fence surrounding the Olympia's ice. I was not especially surprised that Laycoe had aroused an opponent's ire, since that happened with remarkable frequency (it was Laycoe that a furious Maurice Richard chased around the Boston Garden ice in the incident that eventually led to the 1955 Richard Riot in Montreal). Nor was I surprised that Detroit was getting the better of Boston, because this was one of those great Detroit teams of Gordie Howe, Ted Lindsay, Marcel Pronovost and Terry Sawchuk, and they got the better of most teams. But I was astounded that the Olympia ice was surrounded by chain-link fencing instead of protective glass. *A chain-link fence?* Get OUTTA here. That was high school stuff. That one photograph set in my mind forever an image of the Olympia as an old, dark, almost primitive place, an architectural peephole offering a glimpse back at the way the game was played before I began following it.

As with Madison Square Garden, I made what amounted to a pilgrimage to the Olympia, viewing its exterior but never getting inside.

In the summer of 1966, between my junior and senior years at Boston University, I was an intern in the PR department of Chrysler Corporation's Dodge Division Racing Team. I was based in Detroit, though I spent much of my time traveling to races to write stories about factory-sponsored cars and drivers. My colleagues and I were entitled to use the executive dining room, wherein, as racing buffs and gearheads, we were about as welcome as Hell's Angels at the church supper. This is why we often took to eating lunch at the Lindell AC, one of the country's first true sports bars. Formica on the tables. Sports photos on the walls. Cold beer on tap. Unpretentious. Very Detroit.

One hot summer afternoon when the talk had turned from sports in general to hockey in particular, I asked where the Olympia was located. One of the full-timers told me it was on West Grand Boulevard. A fellow writer and I decided to stop there on our way back to the office.

There was a kind of deliberate architectural solidity to the Olympia's exterior. Long, narrow windows, more decorative than functional, ran two to three stories high and the façade of the building rose to a peak on which was mounted a flagpole. Block letters reading OLYMPIA were affixed to the left wall. The building's blockiness reminded me of the old textile mills of my native New England, sturdy, functional and not admitting of too much light. The Olympia seemed as much a place for working as for watching.

Standing on the sidewalk on that hot summer's day, I imagined the building's interior as I'd read it described in columns by Detroit hockey writer Joe Falls. I knew that the building's only frill was a huge escalator that carried fans and journalists to the arena's highest reaches. I also knew that by the 1960s the chain-link fence had been replaced by glass. Yet in my mind's eye that fencing was and remains an apt metaphor for the city and the great Wings' teams of the 1950s, a hard-working, no-frills, lunch-pail team for a hard-working, no-frills, lunch-pail crowd. Even Detroit's immortal Gordie Howe, he of the size 11 (XXL) gloves and cobblestone fists, played with a roll-up-the-sleeves style. There seemed an almost assembly-line inevitability to his goals. Or, as *Detroit News* writer Paul Chandler wrote following Howe's first game at the Olympia, "he literally powered his way through players . . . to the goalmouth."

I would like to have seen Howe and his Production Line teammates Sid Abel and Ted Lindsay in the Olympia on April 23, 1950, when Detroit beat the New York Rangers 4–3 to win the first of what would be four Stanley Cups in six years. Even better, I wish I'd been in the building in the second period of the April 15, 1952, Stanley Cup final, a game in which Detroit would beat Montreal 3–0 and a night on which a Red Wings fan threw an octopus onto the ice starting a tradition that would continue for the rest of the century. The eight arms of the mollusk were intended to represent the eight wins then needed to secure the Stanley Cup. But all the octopus did on that night was annoy Olympia officials and prompt what has to be the most amusing public address announcement in NHL history:

"Octopi shall not occupy the ice. Please refrain from throwing same." Very Detroit.

* * *

As for the new buildings, let me paraphrase a line from *The New York Times* on the occasion of the opening of the current Madison Square Garden: the new places will have to be warmed by a few more sporting memories before they are worthy successors to the old.

REQUIEM FOR THE CUCUMBER

*Madam, all stories, if continued far enough, end in death,
and he is no true story teller who would keep that from you.*
—Ernest Hemingway, "Death in the Afternoon"

The first rule of life and of goaltending is the same: you've got to play hurt.

Georges Vezina knew this.

On November 28, 1925, Vezina, a Montreal Canadiens goaltender making his 367th consecutive start and playing with a temperature of 102°F while coughing up blood, collapsed at the end of the first period of Montreal's National Hockey League home opener vs. Pittsburgh at the Mount Royal Arena. He tried to start the second period, but collapsed again and was helped from the ice and rushed to a hospital, where he was diagnosed with tuberculosis. He died in his hometown of Chicoutimi, Quebec, on March 24, 1926, at age thirty-nine. A lengthy obituary in the *Montreal Standard* called him "the greatest hockey goaltender of the last two decades." More than eighty years later, he remains one of the most important figures in hockey's most important position, his name synonymous with excellence and durability. And yet he is probably the least-known member of the Hockey Hall of Fame, a man whose career is shrouded by the passage of time, the accidental destruction of archival records and Vezina's habitual silence. In the end he was a tragic figure and a reminder of the way life can imitate goaltending. Which brings us to the second rule of life and of goaltending: no matter how well you try to protect yourself, you're going to get hurt.

* * *

Georges Vezina matters. His career spanned two distinct eras of goaltending. For his first eleven seasons, goalies were not allowed to leave their feet to make a save. From 1922 onward, dropping to the ice to make a stop was fundamental to goaltending and a tactic that would become popularized by the butterfly style of Glenn Hall and Tony Esposito, and would reach its apotheosis in Patrick Roy. Vezina won a Stanley Cup in each era, once in 1916 and again in 1924. He had the league's lowest goals against average three times in the stand-up era (1911, 1912 and 1918) and twice (1924 and 1925) in what we might call the prelude to the modern era. His 1.97 goals against average in 1924 was the first below 2.00 in National Hockey League history. He posted the league's first shutout in 1918, and recorded five shutouts in the 1924/'25 season, this in a day when hockey shutouts were about as rare as baseball no-hitters. The man could play.

He was also the first of the great French-Canadian goaltenders on a list that includes Roy, Jacques Plante, Bernie Parent, Martin Brodeur and so many others that Quebec is to goaltending as New Orleans is to jazz. And Georges Vezina is its Louis Armstrong.

The season after Vezina's death, Canadiens owners Leo Dandurand, Louis Letournou and Joe Cattarinich established the Vezina Trophy to be awarded annually to the NHL goaltender allowing the fewest goals. (That changed in 1982, with the Vezina now going "to the goalkeeper adjudged to be the best at his position," as voted by the league's general managers.) The Vezina Trophy will likely be awarded for as long as the professional game is played, thus making Vezina's name immortal.

* * *

It wasn't immortality but death that surrounded me on May 28, 2004, as I stood in a cold rain at *Le Cimetière Catholique Saint-Francois Xavier* in Chicoutimi, staring at the weathered six-foot granite monument with the cross on top, this marking the grave of Georges Vezina and his wife, Marie Stella Morin Vezina. (Marie also knew something about playing hurt, having borne her husband twenty-two children, only two of whom—sons Jean and Marcel—reached adulthood.)

But I've not come to Chicoutimi, a one-time lumber town on the banks of the Saguenay River about 100 miles northeast of Quebec City, solely to pay homage to a dead goalie. I've come partly because I'm curious about Vezina, a man so silent and uncomplaining he was known as *L'habitant silencieux*. He was so tough he played fifteen consecutive seasons without missing a game and indeed almost died in goal, and was so cool in net that the alliterative sportswriters of the twenties labeled him the "Chicoutimi Cucumber," a nickname I first learned of in one of the few letters my father ever wrote to me. It was in the 1980s (the letter is dated February 21, but no year is given) that my father, nearing retirement and about ready to close his woodworking business, took what I imagine was a slow afternoon to make a list of all the sports nicknames he could recall, 117 in all. He thought I might want to write a story on sports nicknames. I didn't but I kept the letter. There, between baseball players "Sudden Sam" McDowell and Paul "Big Poison" Waner is the name "Georges Vezina, the Chicoutimi Cucumber." My father later said it was his favorite sports nickname. "You don't hear nicknames like that anymore," he said. "Today's players won't stand for it. They're too vain."

I also made the trip because I knew that Vezina's grave would mark for me the confluence of the rivers of French-Canadian culture, Roman Catholicism, goaltending, and death; the first three of which informed and shaped much of my life (I played goal as a youth) and the last of which I begin to regard with growing apprehension and curiosity.

And, frankly, I was there because my other choice was Italy.

"Let's go to Italy for our anniversary and your birthday," Barbara had said a few months earlier. I happened to get married on my birthday (pure coincidence since it was the only Saturday in May the church was available) and we've lately been using the anniversary/birthday combination to rationalize a sometimes pricey May vacation.

"The closest I want to get to Italy is *Dean Martin's Greatest Hits*," I said, not because I have anything against Italy but because I have much against the long, shuffling lines at airport gates and Customs and Immigration counters. I pointed out that this was our thirty-sixth anniversary and a trip to Europe might be more appropriate for our fortieth. Barbara agreed, probably because that's what she was aiming for in the first place. We settled for spending a few days at Quebec City's Château Frontenac, a luxurious, castle-like hotel on a promontory above the St. Lawrence River. Quebec City is a nine-hour drive from our home in Natick, Massachusetts. I think of it as a par-5 to an elevated green with water in front. You can't drive to Italy. I checked.

It was at about this time that ESPN sportscaster John Buccigross, who writes a hockey column on ESPN.com and with whom I occasionally correspond because we both maintain backyard hockey rinks, called my attention to an unusual email he'd received from a fan, one Dominic Simard in Chicoutimi. I've forgotten the main topic of Simard's letter, but not the final paragraph in which he wrote that he worked in a cemetery in Chicoutimi and that "the people I work with have a special job for me. Once a week it is my honor to mow the grass over the grave of the great Georges Vezina." Buccigross thought it was an interesting comment. So did I.

I wanted to meet Simard because I was curious about his obvious reverence for a goaltender so long dead. I emailed him, telling him that I was going to Quebec City in late May and that I would drive to Chicoutimi if he would show me Vezina's grave. He agreed, referring to the grave site as "my little place of peace."

When I played goal as a youth, I was no great shakes, but you don't have to be a star to be in the Goaltenders Union. I played a little club hockey, a little school hockey, a little Catholic Youth Organization hockey and this over a period of seven or eight years. Maybe two hundred games, five hundred practices and 932,719 of my friend Dennis Griffin's slapshots taken in the driveway of my father's house in Winchester, Massachusetts. One of the biggest goals I ever gave up was a shot that sailed past me into the garage, where it crashed through the panes of two storm windows that had been stored there. That unhappy event illustrated another of the great truths of goaltending: a goalie can't win, he can only not lose. I take that merely as a reality of goaltending, and not of life. You can win at life. It's dying that's the hard part.

* * *

I played goal just long enough to develop a lifelong interest in that solitary position and the curious people who play it. Especially a man like Vezina. whose name I'd heard since I began following the game in the fifties and yet a player I knew so little about.

"I'm NOT going to a cemetery in Chicoutimi," Barbara said when I proposed a day trip to Vezina's grave. But Friday morning, the day I was to drive to Chicoutimi, dawned cool and rainy and Barbara put herself on the traveling team. This was before she knew about Route 175, a winding three-laner that undulates north through the mountains of the Laurentides Provincial Wildlife Preserve. There is one lane for northbound traffic, one lane for southbound, and a middle lane that seems largely negotiable should you be willing to negotiate with a lumber truck driven by a French Canadian who thinks he's Jacques Villeneuve. It seemed at times a toss-up as to whether the rain-slicked road would take us to the cemetery or put us in one.

We reached Chicoutimi at 11:45, fifteen minutes before we were to meet Simard, appropriately enough at L'Aréna Georges Vezina, located about a half-mile above the south bank of the Saguenay River, which connects Lake St. Jean with the St. Lawrence.

The front door of the arena was unlocked so we ducked inside, where the first thing we saw was Vezina himself staring at us from a large, framed photo in the arena lobby. Vezina, standing straight up and posing for the photo apparently taken outside a rink, wore the red Canadiens jersey with the "CH" logo on the chest. His goalie pads looked more like cricket pads or field hockey goalie pads circa 1960; his gloves were regular hockey gloves, not the stick glove and catch glove that would enhance the play of goalies of the next era. He held his goal stick—the design much the same as today's—in his right hand. A white toque covered his head and was pulled down to his earlobes. He stared straight at the camera and, like the Mona Lisa, appeared to be on the verge of a smile. He looked like a peaceful, quiet, self-contained man. Dignified. Cool as a cucumber.

Dominic Simard arrived a few minutes later, driven to the rink by his father. We were surprised to learn that Dominic was only nineteen years old and working in the cemetery was his summer job. For the rest of the year he was a student at Cégep de Jonquière, a local technical school, where he majored in radio and television. He also played left wing and center with a local amateur hockey team and worked in security at the arena for the games of the Chicoutimi Saguenéens, the local entry in the Quebec Major Junior Hockey League.

"Georges Vezina brings a kind of spirit here," said young Simard who speaks fluent English with a French accent. "Without him," he said, nodding toward the photo, "the rink where we are standing would probably be the South Civic Sports Arena."

"I like him," Barbara whispered to me about Simard as we walked to the car.

With Simard in the back seat navigating—"*gauche* . . . LEFT, I mean. Sorry."—I drove to the cemetery and parked beside a utility shed about 100 feet from Vezina's grave.

"This is it. This is my special place," Simard said.

Standing under Barbara's umbrella and staring at the grave marker, I was reminded less of hockey than of the obligatory Memorial Day visits to the cemetery made with my father, sister and aunt, this to say prayers at, and place flowers on, the graves of relatives. I didn't enjoy making those trips, yet I felt it was a good thing to do. But that was back when I—an altar boy for eight years and Catholic school student for nine—viewed death as the Sisters of St. Joseph and the parish priests told me to view it: as the gateway to a deservedly happy afterlife and a just reward for enduring the travails of this world. Later I would come to see death as the end of all I've ever known and the frightening portal to eternal nothingness. Death bothers me. Death and a sixtieth birthday bothered me a lot. I remembered a line from Emerson. "Already the long shadows of untimely oblivion creep over me." Like most of us, I'd dealt with mortality by whistling past the metaphorical graveyard.

About a year earlier I'd been joking with Barbara and some friends about what we'd have engraved on our tombstones. GAME OVER, I suggested for mine. Barbara said she wanted GAME MIS-COUNDUCT, which my friends and I thought appropriate because Barb is the acknowledged leader in career penalty minutes on our backyard rink.

Now, in Chicoutimi, I deal with my anxiety by making a lame joke. "Everyone in here would like to swap places with you," I say to Barbara, who ignores me as she shifts her camera bag to keep it under the umbrella.

Simard tells us that he often finds little mementos left by visitors to Vezina's grave. "Twice I found pucks with the Montreal Canadiens logo on them," he says. "And sometimes people leave flowers. Who leaves them? This I do not know."

The rain abates for a few minutes. I take off my hat and drape an arm around the gravestone while Barbara takes a couple of photographs. But within minutes the rain picks up again, harder this time, and we sprint to the car and drive off to lunch.

The waitress at a local sports bar speaks little English and I speak even less French, so Simard orders for us. I'm embarrassed at not knowing more than a dozen or so phrases and perhaps a few hundred words of my maternal grandparents' language. I have some audiotapes and a French/English dictionary and I'm trying to learn French, partly in an effort to recapture my culture and partly because I don't want to be the ugly American. But I think I am not trying hard enough.

Simard, Barbara and I talk about hockey and the then-looming NHL lockout. I try to bring the conversation back to Vezina. But Simard, while possessing a great reverence for Vezina, knows little about his career and says only that in Chicoutimi "he still lives in everyone's memory."

Alas, he lives in very few libraries or files. There are two reasons we know so little about Vezina: first, his final game was more than eighty years ago, so there is virtually no one who remembers seeing him play; and second, in 1968 workmen remodeling the Montreal Forum accidentally destroyed some of the team's archives including a file on Vezina. The most significant body of information on Vezina—and it doesn't amount to all that much—is in the archives of the Hockey Hall of Fame in Toronto.

* * *

Six weeks after visiting Chicoutimi, I drove to Toronto to delve through those archives and to learn what I could about the "Chicoutimi Cucumber." In the interest of full disclosure, I also timed the trip to avoid a bridal shower. *Merci, Georges.*

* * *

Vezina was born in Chicoutimi in January 1887, the son of Jacques Vezina, who was the town baker and an immigrant from the village of St. Nicholas de Larochelle in France. When Jacques' business prospered, he bought the local outdoor hockey rink, where Georges had been playing goal not on skates but in boots, a fairly common practice at the time. Because boots offer no ankle protection, a save made by turning the foot sideways would lead to a broken or badly bruised ankle. Thus, Vezina learned early to let his broad-bladed goal stick do most of the work, He didn't start playing goal on skates until he was eighteen and by then he was so adept at kicking out shots that for the rest of his career he reportedly stopped more shots with his stick than with his leg pads or gloves.

Vezina became so good that in 1910, when he was twenty-three and playing for the Chicoutimi town team, he turned in a 60-save shutout in a 1–0 Chicoutimi win over the touring Montreal Canadiens, who immediately did the sensible thing and offered Vezina a contract at $800 a season. Georges, who was engaged to be married later that year, also did the sensible thing and took the money. (The most he ever made from the Canadiens in one season was $3,700.)

Georges joined the Canadiens for the 1910/'11 season and immediately carved about three goals per game off the National Hockey Association (forerunner of the NHL) goals-allowed average. He played all sixteen games, finishing with a 3.90 goals-allowed average in a league where, the season before, the average of all goaltenders was 6.46 and wherein one goalie, Vezina's predecessor, Ted Groux, recorded a stratospheric 8.56.

Vezina played goal the way Fred Astaire danced—from the waist down. One of the few eyewitness accounts of Vezina's style comes from Frank Boucher, who played for the Vancouver Maroons in the 1920s and who faced Vezina several times. Long after Boucher's career was over, he said of Vezina: "I remember him as the coolest man I ever saw, absolutely imperturbable. He stood upright in the net and scarcely ever left his feet; he played all his shots in a standing position. . . . He was remarkably good with his stick. He'd pick off more shots with it than he did with his glove."

There is one grainy, flickering film that shows Vezina practicing with the Canadiens at an outdoor rink. During breaks in the action, Vezina would stand upright and lean on his stick in a pose of passive defiance later made famous by Ken Dryden, Montreal's great goaltender of the 1970s.

In 1979, Robert Ronchon, then eighty-two, a man who had seen his first Canadiens game as a fan in 1914 and watched Vezina play many times, told writer Dave Dunbar of the now defunct *Hockey Magazine* that Vezina wouldn't merely stop a shot with his stick blade but would often kick the blade of the stick, thus directing the puck to teammates. But if Vezina's game was often spectacular, his personality wasn't. "He was a humble, slow-talking man, like a lumberjack," Ronchon said. "He didn't speak English very well and at that time most players were not from Quebec [so] he was quiet. Like an outsider. In a way I guess he was [an outsider]. In those days Chicoutimi was at the end of the world."

* * *

Today Chicoutimi, and most of Quebec beyond greater Montreal, is not so much the end of the world as a world unto itself. At lunch with Simard, Barbara—my warning nudges under the table notwithstanding—raised the question of Quebec sovereignty. (I'll say this for Barb: she goes hard to the net.) The question of Quebec someday breaking away from the rest of Canada and becoming a separate country is a sensitive issue in the province and I'd hoped to avoid the topic. I'm not a big fan of political conversation (when was the last time you changed someone's mind on a political issue?), and I then believed that the 1995 provincial referendum on separatism, which failed by less than 1 percent of the popular vote, was the high-water mark of the separatist movement and that, since then, the tide of public opinion had been going out. I'd thought that the only ones clinging to the idea of Quebec sovereignty were older French Canadians who remembered the day when the province was, in the words of the late Parti Québecois separatist leader René Lévesque, "nothing more than an internal colony which lives at the will of (the English)." But Simard told Barbara that he favored sovereignty. "I'm for it," he said. "And so are most of my friends . . . It isn't strictly about language, it is about a culture that may be lost. Don't get me wrong. I'm proud when Canada wins a World Cup or an Olympic medal. But I'd be proud if it were Quebec."

That surprised me. Not the opinion itself, but the sincere expression of it by one so young. The tide may be going out, but watch out for the undertow.

There was no separatist movement in Vezina's time. And it's unknowable where Vezina would stand on the issue if he lived today. But a newspaper clipping I found in the Hall of Fame archives suggests that Vezina—a man who lived in the dark days of Anglo-Scottish commercial domination—held a more nationalist view and saw sport as a great unifier. In a guest column written for a French-language newspaper in 1923 and translated by Leo Dandurand for the Montreal *Gazette*, Vezina wrote:

> *Every thoughtful Canadian is striving for UNITY [emphasis Vezina's]. That sport, more than anything else, will bring this about was never brought home to me more forcibly than last year in our training camp in Grimsby, Ontario. I, a French Canadian from 700 miles below Quebec, as many are wont to describe Chicoutimi's geographical position, unable to speak English, [working] amongst men of different creed and personality, made fast friends, [people] I would never have known if not for my connection with sport. Sport brings about similar cases . . . every day and easily replaces conferences, speeches, clergy, politicians, etc. as a nationwide [unifier]*

He may have been right about conferences, speeches and politicians but, about the clergy, he was most profoundly wrong. The priests did not care about unification. They cared about power.

In Vezina's day and until late in the last century, the Catholic clergy virtually ran the lives of French Canadians. And one of the main social and political tenets the clergy supported was *la revanche du berceau*. "The revenge of the cradle." What France lost to England on the Plains of Abraham in the 1759 Battle of Quebec, French Canadians would win back in the birthing room, or so the theory went. By populating the country with millions of French Catholics, the French could ward off English assimilation and provide the Church of Rome with an army of new souls. Among French Catholics—a group that included Georges and Marie Vezina—any artificial means of birth control punched your ticket to eternal damnation.

That's standing 'em up at the moral blue line.

That type of arrogance is one of the forces that slowly pushed me away—and keeps me away—from the Church of my childhood and adolescence. I can't imagine Barbara and me subjecting ourselves to such hard-line authority. But, in Vezina's day, millions did.

A thumbnail biography of Vezina handed out by his family at his funeral reports that in the first two years of their marriage Marie Vezina twice lost triplets during or shortly after birth. That she would similarly lose fourteen more children shocks us today but, and alas, it was not all that uncommon at the time.

Georges played in a Stanley Cup final on March 25, 1924, the night his son Marcel was born. Arriving home in Chicoutimi the next day, Vezina celebrated the birth and the Cup by giving the child an English middle name—Stanley. Two years less a day later, Marcel Stanley's father would be dead.

Leo Dandurand could see it coming.

When Vezina reported to the Canadiens' 1925 training camp, he looked gaunt and tired. He also played poorly, prompting Dandurand to sign Alphonse "Frenchy" Lacroix as a backup goalie, this notwithstanding Vezina's assurances that he would play well once the regular season began. Wasn't a little cough and weight loss just another hurt to play through?

Vezina tried to make good on his promise, but then came the collapse on the ice and the trip to Hôtel Dieu, the Montreal hospital where Vezina stayed for a week and was given the diagnosis that in those days was a death sentence. Dandurand visited Vezina daily and honored the goalie's request that the team not be given the details of his sickness. "Perhaps they will play better if they think I am coming on. When I am not on they will soon forget about me in the excitement of the play," Vezina told Dandurand in what the owner and coach called the goalie's "last act of devotion" to the Canadiens. But there was one more act coming. The Canadiens had a practice on the day that Vezina was released from hospital. Vezina's doctor had ordered him to return to Chicoutimi immediately. But first Vezina went to the rink, where in a scene Dandurand later recalled for the *Montreal Standard*:

> *Vezina reported at the usual hour at the dressing room yesterday morning and sat down in his usual corner. . . . I glanced at him as he sat there and saw tears rolling down his cheeks. He was looking at his old pads and skates that [team trainer] Eddie Dufour had arranged in Georges' corner thinking probably that Vezina would don them.*

Eddie Dufour thought wrong. Vezina, who had lost thirty pounds since the start of training camp, would never wear his pads again. Dandurand reported that when Vezina stood to leave the room, "He asked one last favor. The sweater he wore in the last Stanley Cup series. Then he went. That was the last I saw of my friend Georges Vezina."

Vezina died a painful death. According to A.J. Vezina (Georges' great-grandnephew, who said in an interview I found at the Hockey Hall of Fame), every day after school Georges' eldest son Jean would rush to the hospital to see his father, "It was a horrible sight [Jean] saw," A.J. said. "It took [Georges] five months to die."

Three months after Vezina's death, the ten-thousand-strong crowd at a play-off game between the Ottawa Senators and Montreal Maroons at the Montreal Forum observed a moment of silence. A band played "Nearer My God to Thee."

* * *

After lunch in Chicoutimi, Barbara and I drove Dominic Simard to his home before turning and heading back to Quebec City. I was still thinking about the graveyard.

"I think I want to be cremated," I said.

"Great. I'll have this big urn of ashes—like the Stanley Cup—in the living room," said Barbara, who obviously didn't like the idea.

"Scatter them in the yard where the rink is," I said. "Deep end. Down by the net."

"If we don't have you, we won't have the rink."

"Any skating pond will do," I said.

"You're not doing very well with this sixtieth-birthday thing. Sheesh," she said before adding—sincerely, I think—"At least you're finally thinking about some of this stuff." Then, after lowering the backrest of her seat and using her raincoat as a blanket, she was soon asleep.

I kept thinking about religion, death and the possibility of an afterlife, something one is naturally inclined to do when driving Route 175. Nearer My God to Thee, indeed.

That night and the next we dined at two of Quebec City's superb restaurants—*Le Continental* and *Le Saint-Amour* (try the lobster, it's the best in the city)—and wound up our night at *L'Emprise*, a jazz bar at the Hotel Clarendon. This vacation was supposed to be a birthday/anniversary celebration, so I talked no more of graveyards and dead goalies.

On Sunday morning while taking my usual solitary walk around the city, I happened to pass the *Notre-Dame-de-Québec* basilica-cathedral, where people were shuffling in for Mass. On a whim I joined them and took a seat in a back pew on the right side. This was the first time in years that I'd been inside a church for reasons other than weddings or funerals. The service, sermon and singing were in French. Didn't matter. Sitting there amid the flicker of votive candles, and the familiar smell of incense still detectable from some long-ago service, I felt steadied. Comfortable. Connected to part of my past.

I later found out this was the oldest parish church in Quebec, first established in 1647 and rebuilt three times. I wondered if some of my maternal forebears, who first came to the Quebec City area in the seventeenth century, had sat in one of the earlier versions of this church. Said the same prayers I said. Heard the same songs.

I had no desire to go running back into the arms of a Church that probably wouldn't be all that happy to receive me. But I began to wonder if religion could be taken *à la carte* instead of *table d'hôte*. For ten years Barbara had been a social worker with Catholic Charities. She worked with abused and neglected children of any and all faiths and races and—much tougher—with the parents and guardians who had done the abusing and neglecting. I admired that work as I admire the hospitals and schools maintained by the Church. I admire the values of love and compassion that drive such work. But can I possess the one side, love and compassion, without the other—the arrogance of dogmatic authority? Like those modern athletes my father had described as "too vain" to accept nicknames, I wondered if I'd been too proud of my agnosticism, my counterpunch at a Church too proud in its supposed infallibility.

There was no blinding flash of epiphany that morning. And I've been back to church only a few times since. (As actor Dan Aykroyd says: "I slip in the back door a couple of times a year. I like the music.") But that old French basilica on that Sunday seemed a good place to start thinking about finding my own path to spirituality. About filling the void left by a faith abandoned but never replaced. About dealing with mortality by methods other than humor and fear. I think I have years of work to do here. But going to church was the first step. And it is another rule of goaltending and of life that you can play only the next shot, not the whole tournament. I think I made the save. And I'm still in the tournament.

Merci, Georges, mon ami. Merci beaucoup.

MUCH OF WHAT I KNOW ABOUT LIFE I LEARNED TENDING GOAL

He who learns must suffer.
—Aeschylus

The goalie pads are 26-inch Vaughn VPG 400s and the chest and arm protector is a Vaughn Legacy 550. They're youth-size pads and are lighter and better than anything I ever wore. About a year ago, a friend and senior-league goaltender whose sons had outgrown the pads gave them to me to pass on to my grandson Demetre, then aged seven. My friend had seen my grandson on my backyard rink one Sunday afternoon, a day when Demetre had briefly fallen under the spell and tutelage of a visiting high school goalie. Demetre seemed eager to play goal, albeit in a no-lifting game. At first I looked forward to giving my grandson the pads. Then Barbara asked a good question. "Are you *sure* you want to give him those?" she said on the day I discovered the pads my friend had dropped off on my back porch.

The real question Barb raised was the subtextual one: shouldn't a child make an informed *choice* to play goal rather than be steered toward it by an adult? It was a short discussion. "You're right," I said to Barb, and meant it. I took the pads to the cellar, where I hung them on hooks behind an old armchair. The pads are neither hidden, nor are they in plain sight. I've never mentioned them to my grandson.

If he sees them and wants to try them, they're his. And I'd be glad to take some shots on him either in the driveway or on the rink. If he doesn't see them, then perhaps I'm helping him avoid some unhappiness while saving my daughter and son-in-law no small amount of anxiety. As my late father, whose three sons were goalies, once said: "No one suffers like the parent of a goalie." Not unless it's the goalie himself. Better equipment has reduced the physical danger of playing goal, but it's an eternal truth that pucks have eyes and that every goalie will get bruised when that seeing-eye puck finds an unprotected body part or, worse, an unprotected part of the net. Physical hurts are the easy part. Being scored on is worse, and losing a game, especially if the loss is (or is perceived as) your fault, is worst of all. Physical pain goes away, but the memory of public humiliation is a long time subsiding. And box scores are forever.

I don't want to be responsible for my grandson or granddaughter going through what I went through when I first took up the position in the late 1950s. That said, I regard my years in goal, the first three of which were difficult and losing seasons, as among the most valuable and instructive of my life, rather like a stock that has paid dividends for five decades and which dividends I have profitably reinvested in other facets of my life. A few years ago I started to think about what I'd learned tending goal. Then I began to talk about it with Barb in what I think was a preliminary struggle to express the then inexpressible. "You should write it out," Barb said more than once. On a recent morning, while sitting in my car waiting for a custodian to unlock the college building in which I teach, I began jotting notes on the blank side of a memo. I made only two notes that morning but, since then, as I thought more about it, I added one more. Here are three life lessons I learned in the University of the Net, a school of exceptionally hard knocks and priceless enduring compensations:

"You Can Slash Open an Artery and It Isn't Going to Change Anything"

It was a Sunday-morning scrimmage at the old Boston Arena and I was too young to have a driver's license, so my father drove me to the rink and waited through the scrimmage so he could drive us to my grandmother's house for Sunday dinner.

I played badly. I gave up long shots, five-holers, wrong-footers, second chances off sloppy rebounds. I let in everything but the popcorn kiosk. I was still new to goaltending and, in the dressing room afterward, indulged myself in a glove-throwing temper tantrum. This expression of anger was intended to assuage my embarrassment and convey to my teammates the message, wholly unsupported, that I could play better. But it did neither. One by one my teammates packed up their gear and left the arena. I was just getting around to unbuckling my leg pads when my father entered the room carrying the mask that, in my anger and distraction, I'd left on top of one of the goals. "You might want this," he said handing me the mask.

I don't recall my reply, save to say that the tone of it was pouty and angry.

My father, already on his way out of the room, turned and said, "You know, you can slash open an artery and it isn't going to change anything."

My father has been dead for a decade, but that line echoes in my memory. I think the impact of his graphic overstatement and the statement's undeniable truth is what keeps the message with me. Regret is natural to the human condition. We've all done things we wish we hadn't done. But regret is useless except for what we might learn from it. I still regret things but I don't dwell on regret. And from the day my father delivered that line I never again expressed any over-the-top anger in connection with goaltending or with much of anything else. Ralph Waldo Emerson said it more lyrically (if less memorably) than did my father: "Regret calamities if you can thereby help the sufferer; if not, attend your own work and already the evil begins to be repaired."

I was the sufferer on that long-ago Sunday morning. Throwing a catch glove and blocker against a dressing-room wall didn't help. Remembering the bad goals and figuring out what I might have done differently helped a lot. In my early teens I developed a routine where I analyzed my goals-allowed while I made the rounds of my morning paper route. We played on weekends, so Monday was the day I'd drift around my route on auto pilot while mentally replaying the goals I'd given up in our Saturday or Sunday game. I think those analyses helped. And figuring out what I might have done differently was a lot better than getting angry or focusing only on regret.

Today I use a football metaphor for this process. "Breaking down the film," I call it. And while it's been decades since I've had to analyze why a shot beat me, I still use the same process of analytical review to figure out how a lecture, a writing assignment, a relationship or an investment could have been better; and to decide what I might have done, and will do, to make it better. Learning from mistakes is all I can do, regret and anger being unproductive. And slashing open an artery is out of the question, except as the phrase that once helped me learn and now helps me remember.

The Only Shot You Can Stop Is the Next One

As I began to improve as a goaltender, I noticed that I gave up fewer goals in the first period than in the other two periods. In some games it was tough for an opponent to get that first goal. But, once they had it, they'd often get two. And three. And sometimes more. As a game slipped away, I got preoccupied with the score, the time remaining, what defensemen we had on the ice ("Jeez, not the Dancing Elephants again"), when our opponent's top line would take their next shift. I concentrated on everything except my job. I was a spectator not a goaltender.

I eventually learned, as every goalie learns, that to survive in net is to be able to block out all distractions including one's feelings. You shut down your soul if you have to. That was one of the last things I learned as a goaltender, and I think it was the biggest reason that I finally had one magical season when our team went undefeated and won the Greater Boston Archdiocesan Catholic Youth Organization League championship. (In the interest of full disclosure I should also point out that we went unbeaten because we had two lines that could put up numbers that looked like the US Treasury balance.)

Alas, it took me about thirty years before I brought that lesson from the crease to my life. I'm a worrier. And during a period in the early 1990s when I was juggling a full-time college teaching job in Boston, moonlighting as an instructor at a New Hampshire college, taking on multiple magazine assignments and facing the myriad problems that come with having two children in college, I began having migraines and, in general, being unusually anxious even for me. During a phone conversation with my younger brother Patrick, a far better goalie than I was, I launched into a litany of all the responsibilities I was juggling and how difficult I was finding it. Patrick cut me off with one of the hundreds of goaltending metaphors that have passed between us over the years. "Hey, Jack, just play the next shot not the whole tournament," he said.

He couldn't have said it better. It resonated with me because it was something that we'd both learned playing goal but which Patrick, who is more likely to cause migraines than to suffer from them, had carried into the rest of his life, whereas I hadn't. I can't say it changed my life on the spot. It didn't eradicate my tendency to worry. But if I still get butterflies at least those butterflies are flying in formation and toward only one objective and that of my choosing. I don't worry about my 11 A.M. lecture until after my 8 A.M. lecture is delivered. I take life one shot at a time. And I haven't had a migraine in more than ten years.

I deliver my brother's line to my classes as exam time nears and student anxiety soars. I tell them that multitasking is a myth, that they can only do one assignment at a time. The key is to schedule a time for each assignment and then stick to that schedule. I also remind them that nothing relieves anxiety better or faster than getting started. I tell them that when I wrote for a major national magazine I worried intensely as a deadline, and thus the time to stop reporting and begin writing, loomed before me. But, once I sat down to write, anxiety vanished just as it used to once a hockey game got under way. The worst part is always the waiting.

After I say that, I ask if there's anyone in the class who has played goal in ice hockey, field hockey, lacrosse, soccer or water polo. There are often one or two students who played (they're usually the ones who'd smiled knowingly when I gave the class my brother's line). I ask them how they handled the anxiety that accompanies that peculiar position. The answers usually come down to some version of "by going out and playing." That they played one shot at a time is a given. It's the only way you *can* play. It's not the only way we can live, work and think. But it's the best way.

Put in Your Time, There Are No Shortcuts

I recently got an email from a former teammate I hadn't heard from in forty-five years. Jack Kean was a stay-at-home defenseman (note: goalies think kindly of stay-at-home-defensemen and forever wish them well) who was wondering if I'd speak to the Rotary Club in what used to be our hometown. In the course of our backing and forthing via email, he mentioned not our team's unbeaten season but the memory of afternoons shooting pucks off the four-by-eight-foot sheet of plywood that sat in my family's driveway. Rinks were few and practice ice scarce in the early 1960s. We compensated for this by skating on natural ice whenever we could and by taking shots in my driveway when the ponds were un-skateable.

We created a makeshift net by taking a long bamboo pole, the type that carpets used to be rolled on, and laying it across the open garage door by wedging it into the metal tracks that the garage door slid on. I then draped a heavy blanket over the pole and positioned a trash barrel on my left to mark that side of the goal. The edge of the garage served as the right-hand goalpost. I then put on a pair of steel-toed work boots and my goalie gear and let my friends blast away. The garage was made of metal (some combination of steel and aluminum), so pucks flying over the blanket-draped pole put smudgy dents into the inside of the garage's back wall, not to mention on the side of the lawn mower, the handles of garden tools and anything else my father had stored in there. Any shot missing low to my stick side further dented the garage's badly puck-scarred door frame.

The garage was a dented, paint-chipped mess. My father was a patient man where hockey was concerned.

While I'd for many years faced shots in my driveway, it wasn't until I was sixteen that it became almost a daily habit. Sometimes only one guy would show up, most often Dennis Griffin, who had a cannon of a shot but no idea where that shot was going. (Dennis would later become a prominent orthopedic surgeon, in which occupation I trust he controlled his scalpel with more precision that he did his old straight-bladed Northland Pro Lie 7, a weapon of mass destruction where garages and goalies were concerned.) On other days, four or five guys might show up and I'd face hundreds of shots. Sometimes a couple of teammates would stand on either side of our makeshift net, where they would redirect shots coming at me and howl like wolves if a deflected shot billowed the blanket behind me. "Very professional," defenseman George Nowell used to say of any goal that billowed the blanket. (In one memorable street hockey game, Nowell decreed that only "professional" goals would count and that he was the sole arbiter of what was stylish enough to be adjudged a "professional" goal. No one argued. George was the biggest guy on our team.)

I think it's no coincidence that the one good year I had playing goal was the same year in which I must have faced about ten thousand extra shots in my driveway. I got hurt on several dozen of those shots; indeed, I got bruised a lot more in my driveway than I did on the ice. But it was worth it. I didn't regard afternoons in the driveway as "practice" and certainly didn't regard them as work. It was fun. And it was also hugely productive. Something happened in that driveway that embedded the fundamentals of goaltending in muscle memory. I improved by playing and that improvement carried over to the rink. Shots that used to handcuff me became routine saves because I'd stopped similar shots hundreds if not thousands of times. With better play came more confidence and with more confidence came better play. It was a wonderful season, part of the foundation of which was formed in my driveway. We paid the price. We put in our time. We got what we wanted.

* * *

Coda

In late August of 2007 I went back to Winchester, Massachusetts, to attend the wake of a man I'd once coached and whose team won the Boston CYO League championship five seasons after the team I played on had won it. The funeral home was on Washington Street, about four blocks from my old home, long since sold. It was late afternoon when I left the wake and decided to walk back to my old house, thus traveling the route I'd taken through eight years of grammar school, four years of high school and countless trips to Winchester Center stores and to the railroad station.

During that walk my mind was awash in nostalgia. There was the Catholic grammar school, St. Mary's, in which I'd attended Grades 1 through 8 . . . the red-brick nineteenth-century parish church in which I'd served hundreds of Masses without mastering the Latin version of the Apostles' Creed. There was the home of my first date . . . and, farther on, the home of a girl I'd taken to a Bruins game. And at the end of the walk stood the house my parents had bought in 1950. I took a perverse pride in the fact that the front lawn and shrubbery looked scruffier than when I was the unofficial groundskeeper in zealous pursuit of which role I often cut the backyard horizontally for touch football but diagonally in what were the end zones (very professional).

I walked in front of the house as far as the driveway, which was empty of cars. There at the end of the driveway was the same old garage, cluttered and badly rusted but still standing beneath the old silver beech tree, big when my friends and I played under its branches, enormous now. I stared down the driveway and, on the low stick-side corner of the garage, saw the dents put there five decades ago by Dennis Griffin, George Nowell, Jack Kean, George Ross, Dave Hession and a half-dozen others. I could almost hear the crash of a muddy puck banging into the sheet metal, that sonic memory intermixed with recollection of the soft, gratifying THUNK of a puck bouncing off my leg pads or disappearing into my catch glove. I would have liked to walk down the driveway and taken a closer look, maybe crouch in front of the garage one last time. But the house isn't in the family anymore and I didn't want to trespass.

I walked back to my car and drove to my home in Natick, where I parked at the top of my driveway in front of a gleaming white garage door. It is not the original door, the original door having been destroyed (windows shot out, wooden panels split) by our son Brian and his friends. I think the new door cost us about $850. But it's the old broken door that was the true and profitable investment. I trust it's still paying dividends.

* * *

None of this is to say that I'm going to give my grandson or granddaughter the goalie pads hanging on that cellar hook behind the old armchair. But the grandchildren are coming to visit Barbara and me in a few weeks and, before then, I might push that old armchair out of the way.

THE RINK RAT

Work consists of whatever a body is obliged to do. . . .
Play consists of whatever a body is not obliged to do.
  —Mark Twain, *The Adventures of Tom Sawyer*

It is closing in on midnight on a Saturday in 1964 and my friend John Quigley is driving his father's new Plymouth at a steady and then nearly legal 70 miles per hour north on Massachusetts Route 107 across a stretch of seaside grassland called the "Marsh." The Atlantic Ocean is on our right, marsh grass is on our left and rock 'n' roll is on the radio.

For three years we followed this route to Lynn Arena to skate with a group of former high school and youth league players in the 1:15 to 2:15 morning slot. Occasionally John and I drove up early, in hopes of skating with the group that rented the midnight to 1 A.M. slot. It was on such an occasion that, goalie pads buckled together and draped over my right shoulder, I pushed open the red inner doors of the now demolished arena to see the midnight-to-1 A.M. crew skating with only one goalie. An unoccupied net was turned around, open side facing the end boards. I was in a seller's market.

I stood behind the chain-link fence, my goalie pads clearly visible, and let the buyers make the first move.

"Hey, goalie, you want to play?" a player asked.

"Don't have any money," I lied.

"That's okay. We need a goalie."

"You need another skater?" Quigley asked through the fence.

"It'll cost you two bucks," said the player who'd just talked to me.

"That's OK," said Quigley, turning to me. "Loan me two bucks, will you?" There may be honor among thieves, but there was never much of it among rink rats.

In the four or five times a year we skated with the early group and in the two or three times we skated with the guys who had the ice after our group, this being the 2:30 to 3:30 A.M. slot, Quigley and I were never anything but "goalie" and "kid," as in, "Nice save, goalie." Or, more often, "Jeez, goalie, you shoulda had it." For Quigley, who had been an interior lineman with the once formidable Charlestown Townies Park League football team, the remarks were usually, and deservedly, along the lines of "Hey, kid, watch it. This ain't football." But we didn't care. We weren't there to make friends. We just wanted to play.

* * *

I was a rink rat and one of the last of the breed, or so I thought, my belief conforming to generally accepted hockey orthodoxy, which teaches us that there is enough ice and opportunity today for anyone who wants to play. This was not always true. In the days before Bobby Orr spread hockey across the continent, indoor ice was scarce. It was this scarcity that gave rise to a peculiar subspecies of the *genus* hockey player, the rink rat.

The rink rat flourished through the fifties and early sixties, a quiet hammock of time slung between the end of the Korean War and John F. Kennedy's assassination. The rat was a guy (and they were virtually all males in those days) with a seven-day-a-week ice habit, a driver's license, and a military duffel bag or a white laundry sack filled with mismatched hockey equipment, much of it "liberated" from the myriad teams he had played on or dressing rooms he had passed through. The rat believed that sleep is overrated. In the areas where I've lived, north and west of Boston, rink rats were mainly from the so-called hockey towns, Melrose, Arlington, Natick, Charlestown. I've heard that the rat also flourished across Canada and in Minnesota, Michigan and other so-called hockey states.

The breed with which I am most familiar, the Eastern Massachusetts rink rat, usually played for his high school. It wasn't enough. He played in a spring or summer league. It still wasn't enough. The rat craved ice. All the ice he could get. Which is why, Friday to Sunday nights, he haunted the old Boston, Lynn or South Weymouth arenas, his pitch always the same, "Hey, you need another player?" he'd yell to whatever group was renting the early-morning ice. It was always "*need*," never "*want*." The rat was, above all, a hustler.

"It'll cost you a coupla bucks," someone would tell him, this being back in the day when you could rent early-morning ice at $60 for a fifty-minute hour.

"I'll pay you after," the rat would say.

The rat would pay if you cornered him. But rats are hard to corner. The rat came to play, not pay. And if you wanted your two bucks, you had best nail him before he skated his last shift and headed for another rink, his $2 better spent on the staples of a rink rat's existence—coffee and gasoline.

The herding instinct occasionally took over and packs of a dozen or so rink rats would get together to rent the ice for an hour, half of which time would be spent trying to scrape up the rental fee and arguing over sides. Sometimes a pack of rats would arrive at a rink at two or three o'clock in the morning, find the ice unrented and talk the rink attendant down on price, this negotiated fee probably ending up in the attendant's pocket.

Rink rats infesting the Boston area could be found at the old, egg-shaped, spongy-boarded Boston Arena (now Northeastern University's Matthews Arena and much improved), Boston College's now demolished McHugh Forum, or the somewhat patrician Skating Club of Boston, a rink used primarily for figure skaters and one that at one time had a sign instructing those guttersnipe hockey players to "use the rear door."

But hockey was always a backdoor play for the rat, who spent an hour here, an hour there, talking his way into games, conning rink managers and generally going to whatever extremes were necessary to support his habit. These things *had* to be done. The rat was a product of the colliding forces of supply and demand. Organized hockey in my area was in its infancy in the late fifties and early sixties; most towns did not yet have youth leagues, there were only a handful of rinks available for rental, and the school-aged rink rat was then ruled by a principals' association that viewed an eighteen-game, ten-week season as offering enough hockey to sate all but the lunatic fringe. The rat skated through those early-morning hours less because he wanted to (I never really *wanted* to skate at four o'clock in the morning) than because it was the only way he could get enough hockey. The alternative was to attend a boarding school, nearly all of which had their own rinks. But few families could afford to pay the five-figure window sticker at elite academies such as Andover, Exeter or St. Paul's. However, all of this was back before the mountain, or in this case the glacier, came to Muhammed.

* * *

By the early seventies the rink rat was on the brink of extinction, pushed there by a hockey explosion seemingly bent on putting a rink in every city, a league in every town and a child in every new pair of skates. You don't have to hustle ice anymore, kid. Just get the parents to write the check and the game is all yours, twin rinks, paid refs, coaches, home and away uniforms, and scoreboards that work. Want to play in a foreign country? Hop on the bus, Gus. Get on the plane, Jane. Can't play on the travel team? No problem. We have A, B and C teams in A, B and C leagues. Want to skate in the summer? Take your pick of the day camps, overnight camps and summer evening leagues. Welcome to organized hockey, kid. What? How much does it cost? How much you got?

In the mid-to-late sixties with the expansion of the NHL from six teams to twelve and with the arrival in Boston of the incomparable Bobby Orr, entrepreneurs began building private rinks while municipal governments floated bonds for the construction of public rinks. In my area, Massachusetts state government went predictably bananas. The Department of Natural Resources built eighteen rinks, while the Metropolitan District Commission kicked in with twenty-six more. Supply began to exceed demand and the rink rat, like almost everyone else in hockey, was sopped up in the organizational sponge to be wrung out into rules-enforcing, schedule-following, pay-in-advance leagues. The hustler with the duffel bag faded away, driven to extinction by the same economic forces that had created him, supply and demand. Or so I thought.

One shrewd old-timer who didn't think so was the late John "Snooks" Kelley, who coached Boston College hockey for thirty-six seasons. He was the first US college hockey coach to reach 500 wins, retired with a 501–243–15 record and led Boston College to the 1949 national championship. He did this mainly with rink rats.

Kelley died in 1986 but, seven years earlier, I'd sat with him in his windowless office at the old Boston College rink. I was interviewing him for a book I was writing. We talked about the rink rat. The subject inspired Kelley and . . . well, there was no stopping the Snooker when he grabbed the conversational puck and wheeled up ice; two sentences and he was in full filibuster mode. It wasn't really a conversation: Kelley talked, I took notes. I can still hear him speaking in a voice that rumbled up from the lower lobby of his chest and checked out through a mouth set in a face that looked like a topographical map of Ireland.

"My life in hockey [was] not two sets of homes and two sets of aways," he said. "We started Boston College hockey in [the 1930s] with no rink, no sticks and no scholarships. Whatever success I had in coaching was due immeasurably to the kind of boy you could call a rink rat. . . . The term 'rink rat' may mean different things to different people, but to me it always meant anyone who would skate at any hour of the day or night." Rink ratting, Kelley recalled, literally began in the pits.

"Before we had many rinks there were countless pits on construction sites where they were building these housing developments. You'd find kids playing hockey in the pits even before the ponds froze. My whole career was built on that type of kid," said Kelley, whose Jesuit employers skimmed off the hockey-playing cream of Irish-Catholic Boston, including one Tom "Red" Martin, an all-America defenseman who played most of every game for the Eagles from 1958 to 1961 and who Kelley remembered as "a classic rink rat."

"When Red was in high school, he skated more at Harvard than a Harvard varsity player," Kelley recalled. "He lived near the rink and knew the manager and the schedule. When the ice was free, Red was on it. It didn't matter what time it was. That's something you can't get across to kids now. If you told a college team they were going to skate at five o'clock in the morning, which we sometimes did in the early days, not only would they look at you like you were crazy, but you'd end up with a very poorly attended practice, unless maybe some of them stopped in from wherever they were the night before."

As to whether the rink rat was even then, in the late seventies, endangered or already extinct, Kelley admitted to being "unlike anyone else in my view of the rink rat. I think there will always be a kid who can't get enough ice. There'll always be that kid who's willing to dig it out and who doesn't think of rewards first. You can't kill the rink rat."

Maybe not. But I'd pronounced the rat dead in a 1979 story in the now defunct *Hockey Magazine.* To me, the rat was as gone as the doo-wop on the radio of John Quigley's father's '64 Plymouth as it roared across the Marsh. You can imagine my surprise when in July of 2007, coming on for three decades after my interview with Kelley, I heard that the rink rat is indeed alive, well and still hustling.

I learned this through my friend Gerry Hailer, a goalie now in his fifties, who told me that his oldest son, Nick, sixteen, a goaltender for the Milton High School varsity, a good public school team, was spending most summer weekdays playing in a two-hour "shinny" session at the Quincy Youth Arena. This was "organized" hockey only to the extent that the rink scheduled the 11 A.M. to 1 P.M. time slot for any hockey players who wanted to show up. There were high school players, college players and the occasional low-level minor league pro. "And goalies skate for the bubble. Free. So it's a good deal for Nick and me," Gerry said.

"I always skated for the bubble," I said. Gerry, who'd done some rink-ratting in his day, laughed at the memory. I told him I wanted to go see some real rink rats and, in an exchange of emails, we scheduled a day we'd meet at the rink where his son plays. In one of Gerry's emails he reminisced about old-time rink-ratting and, in particular, about what he called the "rat-weasel factor," recalling, "the guys who would gladly 'pay you

Thursday' for an hour of ice on Tuesday. . . . I can not begin to tell you how many disputes I've witnessed over those guys who don't pay before the hour, don't pay after the hour, and pretend to have forgotten about it three weeks later. When confronted they'll spew a string of lies as long and stupid as Jake Blues' when he's on the wrong side of Carrie Fisher's gun. . . . They generally pay, though, even if it's after having taken the second or third free toss of a twelve-ounce Bud Light from a cooler somebody else filled and dragged into the locker room."

* * *

It was a hot July morning when I met Gerry in the parking lot of the Quincy Youth Arena. It was too early for players to take the ice, so Gerry and I did what aging rink rats do, repaired to the nearest doughnut shop (let the record show I had a whole-wheat bagel and tea) and talked hockey.

"I have to be careful not to invade Nick's space," Gerry said, explaining that he came to the rink because his son was driving on a learner's permit and Massachusetts law requires that an adult be in the car. "I try to stay out of the rink. I don't want to get in Nick's way. But the few times I've looked in I've been impressed by the players who come here. You get some hotshots out of CM [Catholic Memorial] and BC [Boston College] High, a kid from Holy Cross. It's quality hockey and Nick's down here four or five days a week." Gerry explained that goaltending was frightfully expensive and, with both of his sons playing goal (son Pete at the Bantam level), "sending Nick to Vladislav Tretiak's goalie camp isn't a viable option. I was impressed" (read: proud) "when Nick found this summer shinny thing."

On the short drive back to the rink, I told Gerry of a Saturday in the early seventies when my father had just come off the ice from having run one of his weekend youth hockey clinics. The father of a young player approached my father and asked: "What would it cost to make my son a goaltender?"

"You can make him a brain surgeon for less," my father said.

Gerry laughed and said that was close to the truth. A few weeks later he sent me a spreadsheet he'd done, this estimating goalie equipment costs for one goalie from Mites through high school varsity. The estimates were based on mid-level prices as listed in an online hockey equipment catalog. The final total was $8,750. And that was for equipment only. It didn't include ice costs, team registration fees, or any extras. My father was right, I thought.

* * *

Gerry and I entered the rink lobby, where a man named Francis sat behind a card table on which was a clipboard with a sheet of paper headed SHINNY. A player carrying an equipment bag came in behind us, walked up to the table and signed his name on the sheet.

"Five dollars," Francis said, adding, rhetorically, "Two hours of ice for five bucks. Best bargain in hockey."

It may be the only bargain in hockey.

Inside the rink Nick Hailer was the only goalie. He was facing two shooters. Two more were in the dressing room putting on their equipment while two others sat in the lobby where, in the time-honored tradition of rink rats, they hedged their bet, unwilling to plunk down five bucks until they had determined whether or not there would be enough players for a scrimmage. There wouldn't be.

"Usually there's enough players for two full teams plus two or three spares," Gerry said. "Don't know what happened today."

What I think happened was that it was a perfect beach day and this in a town where the beckoning sands of Wollaston Beach are a mile from the rink. "Got to really want it to be here on a day like this," I said.

On the ice, Nick Hailer is getting shelled with shots. In succession he makes a left-pad save, two stick saves, a glove save, a butterfly save with his right pad, and a blocker save on the rebound. Finally one of the shooters, the kid from Holy Cross, stuffs a rebound in the short side. Nick pops up on his feet and takes more shots, many of them (too many, I think) close-in blasts. After about twenty minutes of this he takes off his mask and heads for the rink door and the water cooler beyond. Sweat runs down his neck and has already soaked through his undershirt and Colorado Avalanche game shirt.

"Only an hour and a half to go," I say.

"Yeah. I'll get about a hundred and fifty shots today."

I tell him it'll be closer to two hundred. I ask how he can take the hammering for so long.

He explains that for the first hour he works on technique, "angles, positioning, stickhandling, and recovering after a save . . . but for that last hour sometimes you're just hanging on, hoping the puck hits you." He picks up his gloves and goes back on the ice for more. I do a quick calculation. One hundred and fifty shots times four days per week times ten weeks of summer is six thousand shots. You can't take six thousand shots and not get better.

"A month ago I was giving up nine or ten goals in the games," he tells me after the session. "Now it's down to five or six." (Those may not sound like good numbers, but they are because no one plays much defense in shinny hockey. A goalie is on his own.)

A few more players straggle onto the ice, but Nick remains the only goalie. "We can do something with five and a goalie," a player says. The players try a few three-on-twos, but play quickly degenerates into the five guys blasting away at Nick. No one's interested in playing defense. Or in the safety of a goalie. Nick, who'd been butterflying and popping back quickly to his feet during the first hour, is moving slower now, clearly tired. But the shots keep coming. It's a few minutes before 1 P.M. when the Zamboni doors swing open. Nick flips up his mask, tucks his catch glove under his arm and heads for the dressing room. On the way he stops to tell me about his glove. "Actually this one is my father's glove. Mine sort of blew up yesterday. I caught a shot and the webbing just flew apart." A lot of things can break on the road to six thousand shots. Nick Hailer's resolve isn't one of them. It's about ten minutes later when Nick, now in street clothes, walks through the lobby dragging his wheeled goalie bag behind him. "You hitting the beach?" I ask.

"Nah. Weight training," he says. "We have a bar and a bench in our yard." I glance at his father. "Only weight training we ever did was twelve-ounce curls," I say. Gerry smiles and gets into the passenger seat. Nick drives.

Two days later I get a lengthy, thoughtful and unsolicited email from Gerry, who'd been reflecting on the changes in rink ratting between our era and his son's.

"Thirty years later and looking back we begin to see what really happened to hockey," he writes.

When I was growing up I remember the photo of a ripped Bobby Hull out on the farm, shirtless, pitchfork in hand, tossing a bale of hay as big as a Holstein cow up onto a bigger pile of hay. To me, that's what a hockey player was back then. He wasn't a guy who came through a college development program. He didn't plan his career from Squirt A through Juniors or college and into the pros. He didn't go to (gyms) on a daily weight-training regimen. He didn't have an agent. He was lucky to have a high school diploma. Back then, hockey was a blue-collar sport, really. Something you did in the off-hours . . . dreams of playing pro were kept in your hip pocket as a possible ticket out of the factory. If you happened to make it, God bless you. It gave a proud assembly line dad something to brag about while he bolted on fenders for a living.

It's not 100 percent like that anymore. But there's still the rink rat to give hockey that blue-collar regular-guy element. You still see the working and civil service classes well represented in the number of police and firefighters who play. But it's far more likely you'll see guys with college degrees. . . . It costs a lot of money to compete in today's rink.

Gerry had written of hockey in general before coming to his eldest son in particular.

I'm pleased to see that my offspring is among those kids who find their own way to play what's become the sport of kings. It takes a little more hustle . . . but when you know you're never going to [attend] St. Mark's you have to do things the old-fashioned way: find some ice, get yourself to the rink as often as possible, and practice what you learned watching Martin Brodeur on TV. Above all, you can never lose the monkey grip you have on your passion or lose sight of your dreams. It's that sort of attitude that keeps the sport alive among those of us who can, must and will do anything for an hour of ice, the player who to this day will gladly answer to the name "rink rat."

* * *

I waited until the third week of August when hockey clinics and a summer camp had moved into the Quincy Youth Arena, pushing out the rink rats. I asked Nick if, in retrospect, rink-ratting and facing six thousand shots had been worth it.

"This was the most productive and rewarding summer of my life because I played shinny," he said. "I stayed in shape, improved my game and can go into the season with a lot of confidence."

Later, and like his father, Nick elaborated via email:

I think people are brainwashed into thinking that the only way to get better is to spend money on camps, leagues, coaches and development programs. [Those] have their advantages. But nothing comes close to just playing. . . . There were days my back was stiff or my shoulder hurt but then I thought about the winter and what I had to do to be ready for my team. I don't think there's any greater satisfaction than being able to go up to your coaches and teammates and say: "I did everything I could to get ready for the season. I played two hours a day every day . . . And I loved doing it."

* * *

It was 2:15 A.M. when the horn sounded, the wide doors in the corner of the rink flew open and the Zamboni roared onto the ice like a snorting bull intent on running us out of the arena. We got the message. John Quigley and I and about fifteen other guys skated to the narrow side door that led to our grungy dressing room. The game in the room was often tougher than the one on the ice. No topic was out of bounds.

I remember the week defenseman Mike McDonald's fiancée dumped him by handing him back a diamond ring. We weren't even sure Mike would show up that night. (I've changed his name because I suspect that even after forty years the memory of that event remains painful and humiliating.)

Most of us were slumped on the dressing room benches stripping off equipment when Mike, the last guy off the ice, clomped into the room. All of us felt bad for the guy. But that didn't stop Quigley from launching into the opening lyrics of a then popular song about a woman taking a diamond ring off her finger because "It doesn't mean a thing."

That was too cruel, I thought. That was going too far. Others must have thought so, too. The room grew quiet. Quigley kept singing softly as if to himself while he pulled strips of white tape off his shin pads. Please stop, I thought, glancing over at Mike, an ex-Marine, who was staring across the room at Quigley. Then I glanced back at Quigley, who suddenly stopped singing, looked up, grinned and said, "How you doin', Mikey?"

Mike shook his head and laughed. "Doin' OK, John," he said. Then we all laughed, at first with relief and then with honest humor.

It was about 2:30 when John and I climbed back into his father's Plymouth for the drive home. Rink-ratting had given us our hockey for another week. Decades later I've come to see that it gave us a lot more.

UNKNOCKABLE

*The search after the great is the dream of youth,
and the most serious occupation of manhood.*
—Ralph Waldo Emerson, "Uses of Great Men"

*She was a registered nurse about to graduate from Northeastern University.
I was an aspiring writer about to graduate from Boston University. We met
at a party on Cape Cod.*

*It was the third Saturday in May of 1967 and Barbara Baldwin and I
had just been introduced to each other at a friend's parents' waterfront house.
One year to the day later we would be married, but we couldn't know that
then. We knew only that we found each other interesting. We talked a long
time while sitting on a sunny back lawn that sloped down toward the shore
of Buzzard's Bay. It was the start of a conversation that has continued for
more than forty years.*

*Hours into that first talk Barbara told me that the person she most admired
was her sister Mary, who is twelve years older and, whom I would subsequently*

learn, is deserving of all the admiration Barbara accords her. "Who do you admire most?" Barbara asked me.

"Jean Béliveau," I blurted out almost before I'd thought about the question.

Even today my answer surprises me. Béliveau was not my favorite player. And I didn't much like the fact that his Montreal teams routinely beat my hometown Boston Bruins. I think if Barbara had asked "Who's your hero?" I would have said Winston Churchill or Abraham Lincoln. If she had asked who my sports hero was I would have said Jacques Plante. But that's not what she asked. She asked about admiration and, without my dwelling on it, Béliveau, the gold standard of gentlemanly comportment, jumped immediately to mind.

I did not have to tell her who Béliveau was. The former Barbara Spelman Baldwin was a hockey fan long before she met me. She knew. And she approved. "You got a lot of points for that," she has said many times when we reminisce about our first meeting.

* * *

It was a Sunday afternoon in late May of 2007 and I was lying on the living room couch half listening to a Red Sox-at-Texas Rangers baseball game and idly flipping through a stack of weekend newspapers that had accumulated while Barbara and I were in Maine for a wedding. I'd take one section of a paper off the stack on the coffee table and scan it before dropping it onto the stack of papers on the floor. I was about to discard the sports section when the bold-faced names of long-retired Montreal Canadiens players caught my eye. Jean Béliveau, Henri Richard, Dickie Moore, Tom Johnson, Jean-Guy Talbot and Don

Marshall are not names one often sees in the sports pages these days. They were the six surviving members (Johnson is since deceased) of the NHL's greatest dynasty, the 1956/'60 Montreal Canadiens, winners of a record five Stanley Cups in a row. The note in the paper reported that the NHL was sponsoring a reunion for those former Canadiens on Friday, June 1 in Ottawa, the evening before Game 3 of the Stanley Cup finals between the Anaheim Ducks and Ottawa Senators.

"Want to go to Ottawa next weekend?" I asked Barb, who was watching the Sox game more intently than I was.

"What for?"

I told her. She said she only had a few days of vacation time left and she was saving them for summer. But I had a week off before the start of a summer sportswriting course I teach. I decided to go. At first I rationalized the expense (a writer must always rationalize expenses) as a cost of doing business. I was toying with the idea of writing a magazine piece on the late Jacques Plante, goaltender on those five Stanley Cup teams, who, on the evening of November 1, 1959, first wore his self-designed goalie mask in a game at New York, thus becoming the most important player at hockey's most important position. I at first thought the reunion of six of his former teammates would give me a chance to recreate the events of that important night.

But I was also moved by nostalgia at the thought of seeing again, and for probably the last time, six men then in their seventies who, when in their twenties, were important parts of the most dominant NHL dynasty I've ever seen. And I did *see* them. I became a fan in 1955, so I was around for the full run of what we in Boston called "The Montreal Express," a team that would blow into town and destroy your team, all the while thrilling you with a wide-open style that earned them their now nearly forgotten nickname, the "Flying Frenchmen." I'm not saying the 1956/'60 Canadiens could beat today's NHL teams. They couldn't. Today's players are bigger, faster, stronger, better coached, better trained and better equipped. The New York Islanders and Edmonton Oilers of the 1980s, the Detroit Red Wings and New Jersey Devils of the 1990s and many other NHL teams, perhaps all modern NHL teams, would likely beat the Canadiens of the 1950s. And of course it's harder to win a Cup today because there are thirty teams (not six as in the Canadiens day) and because today a Stanley Cup champion must win four best-of-seven series not merely two. But, *in their time,* no team was more commanding or more enjoyable to watch than the late-1950s Canadiens.

In their five-cup run *Le Club de Hockey Canadien* never lost an opening game, never trailed in a series, never went to a Game 7, only twice went to a Game 6, were 40–9 in post-season play and 20–5 in the final round. And they did this with an élan and bravura we would not see again until Wayne Gretzky, Mark Messier and Paul Coffey led the Edmonton Oilers on their 1980s run of four Cups in five years.

Twelve men played on all five Cup teams during the Montreal dynasty, the six I would see in Ottawa plus deceased players Maurice "Rocket" Richard, Claude Provost, Bernie "Boom Boom" Geoffrion, Doug Harvey, Bob Turner and Plante. There are constellations that don't have that many stars.

* * *

Six overstuffed red armchairs stand ten feet apart, arranged like small thrones across a two-foot-high dais in a function room on the second floor of the posh Brookstreet Inn and Spa in Kanata, Ontario, a suburb of Ottawa. I am one of about fifty journalists milling around the room at 5:46 P.M. when, through an open side door, in walk the six Canadiens led by ex-captain Jean Béliveau who, at six feet, three inches, is the tallest person in the room. He walks as he once skated, smoothly, a fusion of equine grace and bovine mass. As always with Béliveau every silver hair is in place and I am reminded of former *Sports Illustrated* columnist Steve Rushin's line that Béliveau "is what God would look like with a five-hundred-dollar haircut."

While I at first rationalized my trip to this reunion as an opportunity to do further research on Plante, when I see Béliveau I realize why I'd really driven 458 miles on my own time and dime. I have long thought that Jean Béliveau is the greatest combination of substance and style ever seen in major North American professional sport. Béliveau is what Joe DiMaggio wanted to be.

Béliveau sits in the first of the red chairs beneath a Canadiens *bleu, blanc, rouge* game shirt bearing his name and retired No. 4. The others sit in the chairs in front of their game shirts. To Béliveau's left sit, in order, Dickie Moore, Don Marshall, Tom Johnson, Jean-Guy Talbot and, at the far end, Henri Richard. NHL vice-president of media relations Gary Meagher introduces the former players and opens the room to questions. As the reporters surge toward the dais, Moore, Marshall, Johnson, Talbot and Richard either sit up or lean forward in their seats. Béliveau leans back. He looks relaxed and comfortable as he answers questions from the francophone media, sometimes emphasizing a point with a monarchical flourish of his left hand on the wrist of which a large watch is barely visible beneath the white shirt cuff jutting from the arm of a gray suit. He wears a plain spread-collar shirt and a quiet paisley tie. He wears nothing that would call attention to itself other than by its correctness.

But there is more to Béliveau than the superficialty of style.

Years earlier, after a game at Maple Leaf Gardens, I had a long talk with my friend and then editor at *The Hockey News*, Steve Dryden, a Béliveau admirer since childhood. "Béliveau's unknockable," said Dryden, who went on to explain his use of that word. Years earlier Dryden, his father and two family friends formed an unofficial club they called "The Unknockables." To be an Unknockable one had to be an elite athlete whose life in and out of the arena was above reproach. Election as an "Unknockable" had to be unanimous. Steve said the four men could only agree on four Unknockables: New York Yankees' first baseman Lou Gehrig, British World Cup soccer star Sir Stanley Matthews, Canadian Football League star Hal Patterson, and Béliveau. (I plan to submit Hobey Baker's name, but that story comes later.)

I told Steve I couldn't knock the unknockables, especially Béliveau.

Aside from having seen him play, my only brush with Béliveau came not directly but through my late father. In February of 1973 the Boston Jr. Braves, a Pee Wee team my father coached, were playing for what was then the Grand Championship of the prestigious Quebec Pee Wee Hockey Tournament still held annually at Quebec City's Le Colisée. The Jr. Braves had reached a two-game total-goals final against Ville Emard, a francophone team from a Quebec City suburb. Boston would defeat Ville Emard, thus becoming the first non-Canadian team to win the tournament that is sometimes called the youth hockey version of the Little League World Series. Béliveau was attending the tournament and he had to be pulling for Ville Emard. Béliveau was born in Trois-Rivières, not far from Quebec City where he played senior hockey for the Quebec Aces before he signed with the Canadiens. It stood to reason that he would support a Canadian team, especially a French-Canadian team. But Béliveau came, uninvited but not unwelcome, into the Jr. Braves' dressing room in Le Colisée before Game 1 of the finals. A tape recorder in a team manager's equipment bag caught most of the visit. My surprised father did the introductions: "Boys, this is Jean Béliveau . . . Mr. Béliveau, the Boston Junior Braves."

"Ah, Boston, yes. It reminds me of the many good games we have there," Béliveau said in a voice that managed to be both deep and gentle. He praised the boys for the way they'd played, wished them luck and said that, "in getting to the finals you have already done a great thing." Then he left, his brief visit now preserved on an old-fashioned thirty-three-and-a-third vinyl LP record album I made with some friends as a souvenir for the Jr. Braves players and their families. The visit was a small but gracious gesture of the type that makes up the tapestry of Béliveau's life.

In May of 2000, as cancer-stricken Maurice Richard slipped into a coma, Béliveau got a call from the Richard family that the Rocket was near the end. Béliveau went directly to the hospital to sit at the bedside of his comatose ex-teammate and the man who had preceded him as Montreal captain. Unable to talk to Richard, Béliveau later said in a TV interview, "I stayed with him and held his hand." I wondered then as I do now how many men, especially in this era of the strutting macho professional athlete, would be comfortable saying they had held a teammate's hand. Not many, I think. But it was the right thing to do and Béliveau did it and was at ease in saying so.

Béliveau was the only former Canadiens player to go to Switzerland to attend Jacques Plante's funeral. A few days later it was Béliveau who helped to arrange a subsequent memorial service for Plante in Montreal.

Such is Béliveau's national reputation that twice in the early nineties then Canadian Prime Minister Brian Mulroney offered to appoint Béliveau to a vacant Senate seat. Béliveau turned down the offers, saying that if he were to serve in Ottawa he would want it to be by election not appointment. In 1994 Béliveau became the only ex-athlete to be offered the governor generalship of Canada, this from then Prime Minister Jean Chrétien. Béliveau politely declined.

Béliveau is the longest-serving captain in Canadiens' history (1961 to 1971), and a two-time winner of the Hart Trophy as the league's most valuable player (1956 and 1964). He was voted the inaugural Conn Smythe Trophy as play-off MVP in 1965 and still holds the league record for most final-series points with 62 (30 goals, 32 assists). In his playing days, the only knock on Béliveau was that *Le gros Bill* too often played like Gentleman Jean. But the charge doesn't hold up. One of hockey's lesser-known facts is that until the arrival of tough guy John Ferguson in 1963, the Canadiens' record for penalty minutes in a season was held by Béliveau, with 143 in 1955/'56. Béliveau didn't play soft. But he didn't go out of his way to fight, either. Wayne Gretzky, appearing on CBC-TV's *Life & Times* biography series, described Béliveau as "the first guy who was able to play the game elegantly without having to be rough, without having to fight. In a lot of ways my play was more like (Béliveau's) than anyone's." Gretzky also said of Béliveau: "He was elegant on the ice, distinguished off it."

Such is the crush of francophone writers and broadcasters around Béliveau and Richard that I talk to the other ex-players while casting sidelong glances at Béliveau and waiting for the crowd around him to diminish.

I approach Jean-Guy Talbot, seventy-four, bald and fit in a Mr. Clean sort of way. He was a durable, stay-at-home defenseman who never scored more than eight goals in a season during his twelve years with Montreal, but who played almost every game and got his name on the Cup seven times. Talbot makes me laugh because, forty-one years after the fact, he still disagrees with the NHL rule change allowing a penalized player to return to the ice if his team is scored upon. "We had a good power play with Jean Béliveau, Doug Harvey, Dickie Moore, Rocket Richard [and Geoffrion]," Talbot says. "When you had a penalty you had to stay in the box two minutes and we used to get two goals all the time. So that's why they changed the rule. I think if you get two minutes you should stay two minutes. Like it used to be," he says. But it couldn't stay that way and Béliveau was one of the main reasons. On November 5, 1955, in a game against Boston, Béliveau scored three power play goals in forty-four seconds while Boston's Hal Laycoe sat in the penalty box. Game over. The rule had to change.

I glance to my left at Béliveau but he's still surrounded by French media, so I move on to Tom Johnson, seventy-nine, dapper in his trademark bow tie. Johnson was one of hockey's better raconteurs. We're talking about Jacques Plante's quirks when Johnson laughs and recalls that:

> Jacques sometimes didn't even stay in the same hotel as the rest of us. In Toronto we'd be in the Royal York and Jacques would be up at the Westbury. He said the air in the Royal York bothered his allergies. But Jacques changed everything. Changed the whole position. He was the first one to come out and stop the puck behind the net and leave it a few feet off the boards for [the defensemen] to pick up. You know how much easier that made our job?

It's a rhetorical question.

The crowd around Béliveau begins to thin out. I walk toward his chair, arriving just in time to hear Béliveau shift seamlessly from French to English to accommodate two English-speaking writers who are there ahead of me. I've heard him do this before at league and team functions and have always been impressed by the ease with which he does it.

I'd heard a story that on the night Plante first wore his mask, the players on the bench had lobbied coach Toe Blake on their injured goalie's behalf. I want to ask Béliveau about this. But just as I begin asking the question an NHL official moves in to ask Béliveau to move to center stage, where a group photo of the six ex-players is being set up. Béliveau gets up out of his chair, which the functionary pushes toward the center of the stage. Béliveau is to be the centerpiece of the group shot. I'm sure I've lost my chance to meet him. But Béliveau doesn't follow the NHL official. Instead he leans down to talk to me. I've been interviewing athletes since 1978. I know when I'm getting a hurried or superficial answer, a cliché-filled, first-draft drifting of the athlete's mind, and when I'm being patronized as one often is when talking to superstars. Those are the most common interview realities of a sportswriter's life. But it's not what I get from Béliveau.

The answer to my question is that, no, there was no lobbying of Blake by the players. "Toe [Blake] didn't have a choice. . . ." Béliveau begins and then it's almost as if he's transported back to that night. "You should have seen Jacques, his nose was over here," Béliveau says, pointing first to the tip of his nose, then to his right cheekbone and growing as animated as I've ever heard him. "So Jacques got sewed up and he said to Toe, 'OK. I can go back in but I'm wearing my mask,' and Toe said OK. He couldn't say no. In those days you would have to use the other team's practice goalie. Jacques Plante or a practice goalie?" Béliveau says, shrugging his shoulders. "It was an easy decision."

We talk about Plante for another minute or two and it is I, not Béliveau, who caves to the pressure of the other five ex-players, a photographer and a league official waiting for Béliveau to take his place in the group photo.

The media conference over, I wander out of the room into an NHL cocktail party where a large screen shows black-and-white highlight films of the Canadiens' play-off games from 1956 to 1960. Two of those five Stanley Cups (1957 and 1958) came in finals against the Boston Bruins. I'm looking at the screen surprised at how easily I can identify players from fifty years ago. Bruins Fleming MacKell, Don McKenney, Leo Labine and goalie Don Simmons bring back memories of boyhood nights in the Boston Garden or at home with the radio turned low and the game that I saw in my imagination as real, and almost as enjoyable, as the one being played on the ice eight miles away. The sight of the old Canadiens players brings to mind a combination of admiration and frustration, the latter because in my youth and for years afterward Boston could never beat Montreal in a series that mattered. But with age has come appreciation. I stare at the game film, at the great players from that era, and I remember Ebenezer Scrooge's joyful exclamation when the Ghost of Christmas Past shows Scrooge his once-beloved first employer, "Why it's old Fezziwig, alive again!"

The grainy, flickering film shows a game that is slower than what we see today but more comprehensible for being so. I'm surprised at how often Béliveau has the puck. He skates much in the style of Mario Lemieux or Jaromir Jagr, in long strides, his deceptive speed coming mainly from his hips. There were some dramatic facial expressions in the era before visors and helmets, but not from Béliveau, who skated with blank-faced aplomb, head up, eyes searching for a pass or shot, and stick-handling no more than necessary. He seems so deliberate as to be almost slow as, up on the screen, he moves the puck from his backhand to his forehand and snaps it into the Bruins' net. His style testifies to what so many modern-day players have said af-ter they've watched a game or two from the press box: you have more time than you think you have. Like Howe, Orr, Gretzky and Lemieux, Béliveau had no discernible panic point.

As I watch the films (transfixed to the point that I am ig-noring an open bar and a table filled with hot *hors d'œuvres*) I begin to see Béliveau as one of six Canadiens from the late fif-ties who could play in any era, the others being Plante, Moore, Doug Harvey and the Richard brothers.

About two hundred guests move into a large dining room, where once again there are five empty red armchairs arranged across a stage, in preparation for the question-and-answer ses-sion that will follow dinner. NHL commissioner Gary Bettman steps to a microphone at the front of the dais. Bettman, while not a glib or engaging speaker, is usually forceful and confident. Not tonight. Bettman is a lawyer and a businessman. But tonight isn't about business, it's about hockey, and Bettman sounds stilted and self-conscious as he reads from a prepared text noting that in 1960 Jacques Plante became the first goalie "to remove his face mask to celebrate a Stanley Cup," that these players "laced leather skates" and that we in the room "are truly in the presence of hockey royalty." Bettman is still reading when veteran hockey writer Eric Duhatschek of *The Globe and Mail* whispers to me: "This is as nervous as I've seen Bettman in a long time." Maybe there is too much royalty in the room.

The six ex-players seem to be the only people who are at ease. As they take their places in the armchairs after dinner, Tom Johnson looks at a replica of the Stanley Cup to be given to each player. "A bit small, eh?" he says, then smiles.

The questions from the audience seem somehow careful. Obvious. The answers are less so. Someone asks Henri Richard, who made the Canadiens' roster as a nineteen-year-old, "when did you know you'd made the club?"

Richard shrugs, smirks, waits a couple of beats and says. "Maurice was my brother." The answer gets a laugh and lightens the mood. But Richard's joke is misleading.

Johnson tells a story that at the end of the first week of training camp in 1955, "Toe [coach Blake] called me and a couple of the veterans into his office. He didn't want it to look like he was taking Henri [Johnson pronounces it "Henry"] because he was Maurice's brother. 'I just want to know if I'm seeing this thing right,' Toe said."

"I told him, 'Toe, the kid's had the puck all week.'"

Someone asks Johnson if Plante's aloofness was resented or divisive. The answer says a lot about the values those players shared: "Jacques didn't want to associate with us. But that was OK," Johnson says, "He stopped the puck." Johnson told me later: "In the play-offs he could stop an Aspirin."

The most interesting question is posed to all six players: which of the five Cup-winning teams do they think was the best? Richard and Johnson pick 1956, when the Habs beat Detroit four games to one in the finals with Maurice Richard, who had been suspended for the previous season's play-offs, scoring the Cup winner in a 3–1 win at the Forum.

Béliveau, Marshall, and Talbot pick 1958, a season in which Dickie Moore led the league in goals (thirty-six) and points (eighty-four), Henri Richard led in assists (fifty-two) and Maurice Richard scored the sixth and last of his overtime goals to beat Boston 3–2 in Game 5 of a final series the Canadiens won in six.

Moore doesn't name any one season. "We had the best team in the history of hockey," he says. It isn't a throwaway line. He says it with conviction and pride.

But it's Béliveau, speaking earlier and for the group, who says it best: "I don't know if anyone will ever break our record of five straight Stanley Cup championships. It is a record that I [and] the rest of the players from that era are proud of. It is a great team record. It is one that just may stand the test of time."

* * *

The night after the reunion dinner, the Ottawa Senators play the Anaheim Ducks in Game 3 of the Stanley Cup Final. The Senators win 5–3, but Anaheim goes on to win the Stanley Cup four games to one. I wonder if the Ducks will win four more in a row.

I don't stay for Game 3. After the dinner I call Barbara to tell her I'll be home for supper the next day. She asks what she always asks when I phone from the road: "How'd it go?"

"Brought back a lot of memories," I said.

"You talk to Béliveau?"

"Briefly," I said, adding: "I picked the right guy." We share another laugh at our long-standing private joke.

"Yeah, you got a lot of points for that," she says, as she always says.

Hey, Big Jean, you know those 809 career assists you have? Make it 810.

SEARCHING FOR HOBEY BAKER

His nature is too noble for this world.
—Shakespeare, *Coriolanus*

My father's business was woodworking and interior finishing, but he wanted to be a writer. He had one story published, this in *Turf & Sport Digest*, a horse-racing magazine. I think the story was about a system he had for picking long shots. The system worked so well that my father often hit me up for loans from my paper route money.

Maybe my father wanted me to be the writer he never was. I don't know. I do know that he was a heavy reader. There were piles of books stacked up in every corner of our house, and he'd often give me a book, magazine story or newspaper column that he thought was exceptionally well written. I still remember the morning he reached across the kitchen table and handed me the *Boston Herald* folded so that all I could see was George

Frazier's column. "Read this," my father said. "The man writes like a dream."

Frazier was not a sports columnist and was, therefore, unknown to me, as my father had correctly assumed. It was December of 1962 and Frazier, whom I would soon come to admire as one of the most literate and stylish columnists in Boston or perhaps anywhere, had written his column on a hockey player. Hobey Baker. I'd never read newspaper writing like this. It showed me what I could aspire to, though never attain. That column was one of only two that I ever carried around in my wallet until the newsprint yellowed and fell apart (the other story was a Jimmy Cannon column on Baltimore Colts quarterback Johnny Unitas). My father was right. Frazier wrote like a dream. I recently looked up that old column. Forty-five years after I'd first read it, I found myself as drawn to the subject as I first was to the style:

> It is odd how his name keeps coming up after all these years, the mere mention of it invoking the past so poignantly that, for a little while, it seems almost as if he were among us still, the grace of him making wonderlands of all our winters, he whose gift was to be glimpsed so briefly. But whom the gods love and so forth, nor did that ever seem so tragically true as on that December morning when he perished over an alien land.
>
> Of forty-five years all but two days have fled since then, but the image of him remains as it was in the swiftness and sinew of his youth, when, of all college boys, he was the most golden and godlike . . . the remembrance of him is redolent enough to summon up the sight of

the crowd getting to its feet and screaming "Here he comes!" as he
took the puck from behind his net and started up the ice, gathering
speed until finally his skates seemed a streak of chain lightning and
the Greek-god blondness of him almost a blur, making hearts leap up.
In the magic of moments like that he was more miracle than man.
Nor is this legend, either, for even the most circumspect of hockey
devotees who saw him agree that he was very, very special indeed.
—George Frazier

About two weeks after I'd reread that column—late on the hot, muggy afternoon of July 17, 2007—I pushed open the big front door of the Ohrstrom Library on the campus of St. Paul's School in Concord, New Hampshire. I bounded down the front steps, a manila folder in my left hand, my car keys in my right. At the bottom of the stairs, I turned right toward my parked car. Then I stopped, put my keys in my pocket, turned left, and walked the few yards to the shore of Lower School Pond. I stepped through some marshy grass and dipped the fingers of my right hand into the brackish water. A deep synaptic impulse born of nine years in a Catholic school and six as an altar boy almost had me lifting my fingers to make the sign of the Cross, "blessing myself" as we used to call it. The only reason I didn't do that is that I was afraid someone might be watching and I'd look foolish. Instead I dried my hand by wiping it on the left arm of my golf shirt, and then walked to my car. That moment of spontaneous aquatic reverence came about because Lower School Pond is where Hobey Baker learned to play hockey.

I was at St. Paul's because an old friend of my late father's, John Lorenz, St. Paul's form of '51 (St. Paul's still uses the old

British word "form" instead of "class"), had interceded with the Rector (read: headmaster) and former varsity hockey coach Bill Matthews to get me access to the school's archives, where I hoped to learn more about Baker, whose athletic skills and standards of sportsmanship and character seemed too good to be true and whose death in the crash of the fighter plane he was piloting is still shaded in mystery. Was it an accident or did Hobey Baker, the last man to die in the First World War, take his life?

There have been other great American-born hockey players: Frank Brimsek, Brian Leetch, Chris Chelios, Tom Barrasso, Mike Modano and Joe Mullen, to name a few. But only Hobey Baker has transcended athletic greatness to become a legend, the only American-born player to rank with Rocket Richard, Gordie Howe, Bobby Orr, Mario Lemieux and Wayne Gretzky in the pantheon of hockey's mythological immortals.

I'd heard of Hobey Baker before my father showed me Frazier's column. I'd come across Baker's picture in a book, *Pictorial History of American Sport* (A. S. Barnes Co., 1952), that is now the oldest volume in my modest library. The book was given to me on Christmas 1954 by my late Uncle Bill and Aunt Hazel. I recently dug that volume out of my cellar bookcase. There on page 168 is a 1913 photo of Baker in his Princeton hockey uniform, form-fitting black tights and long-sleeved crew-neck shirt, unpadded white shorts and black skates that look more like figure skates than hockey skates. He has his hands on his hips and is staring, unsmiling, at the camera. He is movie-star handsome with wavy blond hair and a well-defined mesomorphic five-foot-nine 160-pound body (his size being about average in the pre–First World War United States). He looks like a dancer, which, in a manner of speaking, he was. The best skaters always are. Many writers have likened Baker to Adonis, in mythology a young hunter who was seduced by Venus, goddess of love and beauty. Venus fell in love with Adonis and warned him not to hunt big game alone. "Beware how you expose yourself to danger and put my happiness at risk." Adonis ignored her warning. Myth has it that Venus's jealous suitor, Ares, came to earth in the guise of a wild boar and killed Adonis. There are parallels to that myth in the life of Hobey Baker.

The copy beside the photograph in my old book notes that, "Baker was head and shoulders above the college hockey players of his time, as good as any Canadian pro. He was elected in 1946 to the Hockey Hall of Fame . . . the only American amateur to be so honored." (Other Americans have been inducted to the Hall of Fame since then, but Baker is the only American charter member.)

Baker is the only man in both the Hockey and Football Halls of Fame. He was an idol of F. Scott Fitzgerald and a friend of Cole Porter.

"In his day and perhaps forever (Baker) was the most romantic figure in all of sports," wrote Ron Fimrite in *Sports Illustrated* in 1991, sixty-three years after Baker's death.

Even though I became a regular reader of Frazier's column I never bothered to learn much about Baker except for what most hockey fans knew, that every year since 1980 the Hobey Baker Award goes to the best US college hockey player (except in those years when it goes to a very good player whose college has the best sports information director). It is only recently, prompted at first by curiosity and later by growing admiration, that I began to look back on and to think about the life of Hobey Baker. I'd never seen, heard or read of anyone like him. I can barely imagine that such a player and person existed. His story is the most compelling biography in hockey history.

* * *

Hobart Amory Hare Baker was born on January 15, 1892, in Bala-Cynwyd, Pennsylvania, to a prominent Philadelphia Main Line family. His father was Alfred Thornton Baker, who made his money in the upholstery business. The boy's mother was the former Mary Augusta Pemberton, a Philadelphia debutante and socialite. Hobey was named after his maternal uncle, Dr. Hobart Amory Hare, the obstetrician at the hockey-player-to-be's birth.

When Hobey was eleven his parents, their marriage unraveling (they divorced in 1907), sent Hobey and his older brother Thornton, twelve, to St. Paul's School. St. Paul's was founded in 1855 and is one of the oldest and most prestigious private schools in the United States. St. Paul's is also the cradle of American hockey. The game has been played there since the 1870s, when goals were ten feet wide and a team was made up of eleven players. In Hobey's era as many as nine wooden-boarded rinks stood clustered together on Lower School Pond. It was on these rinks that the Baker brothers learned to skate and play hockey.

And it was here that Hobey, when he became an upper class-man, got his house master's permission to skate at night and by playing in the dark—or so legend has it—taught himself to stickhandle without looking down at the puck, a common and essential skill today but rare in Baker's time. Indeed, Baker's plaque in Toronto's Hockey Hall of Fame notes that, "once the puck touched his stick he never had to look down again."

Hobey made St. Paul's varsity at the age of fourteen. Within two seasons he was leading his prep school teammates to wins over the best college teams in the country. In the 1908/'09 season, St. Paul's beat Harvard 5–3, with Hobey reportedly outplaying Harvard's captain and fastest skater Clarence Pell. The next season St. Paul's played Princeton, a team that would win that season's college championship, and beat them 4–0.

John Davies, author of the 1966 Baker biography, *The Legend of Hobey Baker* (Little, Brown), quotes one of Baker's St. Paul's teammates as saying that Hobey "flew over the surface like a bird, doing inner and outer edges in wide arcs. I had seen pros play in Pittsburgh, where I had first played hockey, but I had never seen such speed nor such grace."

Baker also excelled at football, baseball, gymnastics, swimming, diving, cross-country, golf and basically any sport he tried. He could juggle five balls and, later in his life, was proficient at polo and roller skating the first time he tried them. Were he a guest in your house he might well descend to breakfast by walking down the staircase on his hands, such was his balance, body control and apparent desire to express himself physically. He was reportedly the most popular boy at St. Paul's and the best amateur hockey player in the country. Maybe the best player, period.

In 1909, the year of Hobey and Thornton's graduation, their father had to tell them that a succession of financial reversals meant he could send only one son to college and even that would have to be put off for another year. Thornton, to his eternal credit, chose to go to work in the family business and to let his more athletically gifted brother enroll at Princeton.

Hobey stayed an extra year at St. Paul's. On occasional trips south to visit his father, eighteen-year-old Hobey would scrimmage on Lake Carnegie with the Princeton varsity. He was the best player on the ice.

Once at Princeton, Hobey became as big a star in football as he was in hockey. On October 13, 1912, a story in the *Boston Herald* called Baker "the most feared open field runner now playing the game of football."

Princeton won the national football championship in Baker's first varsity season and went 20–3–4 over his career. Baker was a dropkicker who could kick field goals from beyond 40 yards, and a punt returner in a day when teams routinely punted thirty to forty times a game, hoping to capitalize on a punt returner's fumble, a fumble often caused by brutal hits. Hobey rarely fumbled and his unique way of fielding a punt made him hard to tackle. Instead of waiting under the punt, an inviting target for the would-be tacklers running at him, Baker sometimes stood back several yards from where the ball would come down, then at the last moment sprinted toward the ball, fielding it in full stride and leaving a trail of surprised opponents in his wake. He played without a helmet. "His golden hair became his ensign. When joyful spectators cried out 'Here he comes!' there could be no doubting the object of their excitement," wrote *SI*'s Fimrite. The ninety-two points Baker scored in 1912 would remain Princeton football's single-season scoring record for sixty-two years.

Baker was a senior and football captain in 1913 when soon-to-be novelist F. Scott Fitzgerald enrolled as a freshman at Princeton. Seven years later Fitzgerald, writing his first novel, used Baker as the minor character Allenby in *This Side of Paradise*. The novel's protagonist, Amory Blaine, is sitting on the front steps of his Princeton rooming house watching a white-clad group of upper classmen walk by: "There at the head of the white platoon marched Allenby, the football captain, slim and defiant, as if aware that this year the hopes of the college rested on him, that his hundred-and-sixty pounds were expected to dodge to victory through the heavy blue and crimson lines."

As great as Baker was in football he was better in hockey. He played a position called "rover" in the seven-man hockey of the time. A rover, as the name implies, was free to go anywhere on the ice, which freedom meant that Hobey would often skate past the same opponent two or three times during one puck possession.

Princeton teams went 27–7 during his three varsity seasons (freshmen were ineligible for varsity play in those days). Because he was his team's top scorer and best player, Hobey was often hacked, tripped, held, speared and otherwise abused. He almost never retaliated. Indeed, he received only one penalty in his college career, slashing against Harvard at the Boston Arena on January 22, 1913. No matter how bad the abuse or his injuries therefrom, Baker made it a point after a game to visit the opposing team's locker room, shake each player's hand and say thanks for a "good game."

Because Princeton didn't have a rink of its own, the varsity often played its games at New York's St. Nicholas Arena at the corner of 66th Street and Columbus Avenue. Playing in New York brought Baker to the attention of large crowds and widely read sportswriters. Lawrence Perry, a sportswriter for the *New York Post*, wrote: "Men and women went hysterical when Baker flashed down the ice on one of his brilliant runs with the puck. I have never heard such spontaneous cheering for an athlete as greeted [Baker] a hundred times a night."

A few times the marquee of the St. Nick's Arena read: HOBEY BAKER PLAYS TONIGHT. Or at least it did until Baker, concerned about what his teammates might think, made the building's manager take down the sign. Baker disliked personal publicity and rarely spoke to reporters.

After graduating from Princeton and taking a job on Wall Street, Baker joined with other former Princeton, Harvard and Yale players on the St. Nick's Hockey Club. Hobey was still the best player notwithstanding that he was now playing against the best amateur teams in the United States and some professional and semi-pro teams from Canada. Lester Patrick, a two-time Stanley Cup winner (1905 and '06 with the Montreal Wanderers) and later founder of the professional Pacific Coast Hockey League, said that not only was Baker good enough to play pro hockey but that he would have been a star from his first game. In 1914, after Hobey led the St. Nick's team to victory in a series against the Montreal Stars, a Montreal newspaper reported that "Uncle Sam had the cheek to develop a first-class hockey player . . . who wasn't born in Montreal."

Baker had offers to turn pro. The *Boston Herald and Journal* reported that the pre-NHL Montreal Canadiens offered Baker $20,000 to play three seasons. Baker turned them down, probably because in those days it was considered unseemly for a gentleman of Baker's social class to play for money. Instead, Hobey worked at what he considered a boring job as a bond salesman and got his adrenaline fix by skating with St. Nick's in the winter and taking after-work flying lessons on Governor's Island in the summer.

When the First World War broke out in Europe—but before the United States entered it—Baker, like hundreds of other young Americans of his social station, volunteered as a pilot in France's famed Lafayette Escadrille, a unit that would become part of the US Army when American forces went into the war. Baker was what we would today call a fighter pilot, but what, in the war, was called a pursuit pilot. American newspapers often referred to him, inaccurately, as an "ace", a pilot who has shot down five or more enemy planes. That wasn't true. Baker had three confirmed kills and a possible fourth, but that was only because he was at first used as a flight instructor and didn't get into combat until late in the war.

He spent many of his furloughs in Paris, where he was an occasional guest at composer Cole Porter's parties. Paris was where Baker reconnected with Jeanne Marie (Mimi) Scott, a wealthy American socialite whom Hobey had first met in New York. They fell in love (or at least Hobey did) and were briefly engaged, an event much trumpeted in the American press. One newspaper report gushed: "Mimi Scott engaged. Well! Well! The announcement of Miss Scott's engagement to Lieut. Hobart A. H. Baker, U.S.A. aviation corp, came as a complete surprise to society."

Its conclusion came as a complete surprise to Hobey Baker. No defenseman ever hit Baker harder than did Mimi Scott when, a few weeks before the war's end, and after Baker had cashed in a bond to buy her an engagement ring, she dumped him for a wealthy American diplomat. But brevity is endemic to wartime romance.

You say "Hobey Baker" and all of a sudden you see the gallantry of a world long since gone, a world of all the sad young men, a world in which handsome young officers spent their leaves tea-dancing at the Plaza to the strains of the season; a world in which poets sang of their rendezvous with death when spring came round with rustling shade and apple blossoms filled the air.

It was a world in which young men soared into the sky and fell in flames.

—George Frazier

* * *

Baker never went down in flames, but he went down.

On the rainy morning of December 21, 1918, Baker, his army discharge papers in his pocket, was scheduled to take a train from the air base in Toul, France, to Paris and then to board a ship for passage back to the United States. Before he left the base, Baker decided to take one final flight in his fighter plane, a SPAD that he'd had painted black and orange, Princeton's colors. Tiger colors. (Listen hard and you can hear Venus warning Adonis: "Your youth, and the beauty that charms Venus, will not touch the hearts of lions. . . .")

Other officers tried to talk Baker out of flying. They couldn't. Nor could anyone order him not to fly, because Baker was by now the squadron commander.

When Baker got to the hangar where his No. 2 SPAD was kept, he ran into a mechanic who told him that another plane, the recently repaired No. 7 SPAD, which had had a new carburetor installed because the previous one had failed in flight, was repaired and ready for testing. Hobey decided to fly the repaired plane instead of his own. He didn't fly far. Or maybe he flew forever:

> When he was five hundred meters above the field the motor suddenly stopped. They buried him in the rain. . . . Then his men fired three volleys and taps sounded plaintively across the French country side.
> —George Frazier

There was, and there remains, speculation that Hobey Baker's death was a suicide. That he was upset over the recent breakup of his engagement to Mimi Scott, that he considered himself neither suited nor inclined to the business career expected of him, and that without the adrenaline surges of sports or war he had little to look forward to. The truth is unknowable. But I doubt Hobey Baker took his own life. According to biographer John Davies, a new Zenith carburetor had recently replaced an unreliable Claudel carburetor on the plane Baker died in. But, because the war was over, the plane's inexperienced pilot had refused to take the now needless risk of test-flying his repaired plane. So Baker tested it and it failed. Had he been higher he might have had enough space and time to crash-land the SPAD, as he and other pilots had done so many times during the war. But this time he was too close to the ground when the carburetor cut out. He was unconscious when his fellow airmen found him. He died in an ambulance.

Let Venus speak for all of us:

As she drew near and saw from on high his lifeless body bathed in blood, she alighted and, bending over it, beat her breast and tore her hair. Reproaching the Fates she said, "Yet theirs shall be but a partial triumph; memorials of my grief shall endure, and the spectacle of your death, my Adonis, and of my lamentations shall be annually renewed."

—*Bulfinch's Mythology*

Myth says that Venus changed Adonis's blood into a flower—the short-lived anemone. We in hockey changed Baker into a trophy. And a legend.

"It is with emotion too poignant for orderly thought or precise expression that I write of Hobey Baker, whose death last

Saturday, through the falling of his airplane at Toul, has just been announced," wrote Lawrence Perry in the *New York Post.* He continued:

> *I don't think anyone who knew Hobey Baker personally, or as an athlete, will have any feeling other than that he was qualified to stand aloof as the ultimate product of all that is worthy, not [only] in American college athletics, but in American college life.*

At about the same time New York newspapers carried news of Baker's death, they also carried the announcement of Mimi Scott's engagement to Philander Lathrop Cable, Harvard class of 1914. Cable was the man for whom Scott had left Baker. Mimi and Philander divorced in 1937. In 1942 she married Paul Lennon of New York. They later divorced. "I wonder if she ever thought of Hobey," John Lorenz asked rhetorically in a note he sent me about a month after we'd visited St. Paul's. "He was probably well off without her. But maybe he wouldn't have taken that last flight if she hadn't dumped him." That question will linger forever.

* * *

I went to St. Paul's School not thinking that I would uncover anything new on Baker but merely hoping to increase my knowledge of him and to get closer to the source of my deepening wonder. As preparation for my visit, I read again Fitzgerald's *This Side of Paradise,* where, in a paragraph on "New England, the land of schools," Fitzgerald mentions "St. Paul's with its great rinks."

I put off my trip to the school's archives until after lunch so that I could tour the campus with John Lorenz in the morning. One of the first places we visited was the Captains Room, which is attached to one of the school's two indoor rinks. The cavernous lounge is dominated by a large fireplace, many photographs (including one of a team of plow horses being used to clear an outdoor hockey rink in pre-Zamboni days), and a lucite display case containing one of Hobey Baker's skate blades. I was drawn immediately to the blade that a small sign said was a gift from Princeton to St. Paul's in 1960, the fiftieth anniversary of Baker leaving St. Paul's. The silver blade is attached to two plates that screwed onto a player's boots. I couldn't see the bottom of the blade, the edges, except for where the blade curved upward in front. That part of the blade looked sharp.

I'd read that Baker was so particular about his skates that he had them sharpened in Canada and that he owned several pairs with one pair always en route from or to Montreal.

To the left of the display case, there is an oil painting of a man with a pencil-thin mustache who is wearing a white shirt, plaid tie and blue blazer with brass buttons and a crest on the pocket. He holds a pipe in his left hand and appears to be the embodiment of Anglo-Saxon preppy dignity. His name was Malcolm Kenneth Gordon, St. Paul's form of 1887, a longtime teacher at the school and Hobey Baker's coach in hockey and football. Later that day I found a story Gordon wrote for a 1940 St. Paul's hockey program. The story was Gordon's remembrance of Baker:

The writer knew him from the time he was ten years old. . . .
Having coached him in hockey and in football, I can truthfully say
that he was always cheerful and helpful even during the dullest
practice. His enthusiasm was contagious and his joy in the game
was an inspiration to his teammates. He never showed the slightest
resentment even in the heat of a contest and his endurance seemed
almost unbounded.

Gordon then recounts a story that is almost unfathomable to those of us brought up on forty-five-second-shift hockey and two-platoon football. Gordon said the story was told to him by Fellowes Morgan, one of Baker's schoolmates at St. Paul's and Princeton.

In 1911 Morgan traveled to New Haven, Connecticut, for a football game between Princeton and Yale. It was Hobey Baker's first season as a varsity football player. The game was played on a cold rainy Saturday. "The field soon became a mire and the ball was hard to handle," Gordon wrote.

Early in the game, Princeton had scored on a fumble, and during
the remainder of the game Yale kept punting to Hobey . . . in hopes
of recovering [a fumble] and thereby scoring. Yale had a pair of
outstanding ends who were down[field] on every punt and threw
Hobey heavily before he could get started. No back ever received
severer punishment, but Hobey never dropped that slippery ball, and
Yale never scored. After the game Hobey dressed quickly . . . and ran
to the train to New York. Morgan happened to [meet Baker] . . . and
after congratulating him asked why he was in such a hurry. [Baker
said] "this is the opening night of the St. Nicholas rink, and I'm
hurrying back to town to get on my skates."

Hours after playing sixty minutes of a brutal college football game, Baker played an entire game of high-level amateur hockey.

In his senior year at Princeton, Baker played all seventy-three minutes of a now famous game against Harvard in January 1914 at a sold-out Boston Arena. The game was 1–1 after forty minutes of regulation, ten minutes of overtime and twenty-three minutes of sudden death when a tall, lanky Harvard substitute, a future U. S. Senator from Massachusetts, scored the game winner for Harvard.

> And to have played with or against him, ah, that must have been something; and as for having defeated him, well, there is a man who on a night in 1914, came out on to the ice and scored the goal that was to win for Harvard. . . . Now that man is full of honors and fame, for he is Leverett Saltonstall, who, on winter mornings, sometimes plays hockey with his grandchildren, and always the stick he uses is the one with which he scored the goal for Harvard over Hobey Baker.
> —George Frazier

I follow Lorenz into the Chapel of Saints Peter and Paul, where Baker and all St. Paul's students had to go eight times a week, once daily and twice on Sunday. An organist, unseen beneath tiers of keyboards, is playing a hymn unfamiliar to me but dirge-like in tone and volume. The music seems an appropriate soundtrack to what first catches my eye. To the left of the main chapel entrance there is a large marble statue of an angel, its arms around a wounded boy whom the angel is about to bear into heaven. Flanking the statue to the left and right are two rows of twenty-four names each. They are St. Paul's alumni who died in the First World War. The top name in the left-hand column is Hobart Amory Hare Baker. A plaque with a quotation from St. Jerome, Epistle 53, reads: LET US LEARN THOSE THINGS ON EARTH, THE KNOWLEDGE OF WHICH CONTINUES IN HEAVEN.

Apparently one of the first things a St. Paul's student learns is the nobility of sacrifice. On the way to lunch with Lorenz and Rector Bill Matthews, we stop by a plaque of the form of 1909. Hobey and Thornton Baker are listed among the sixty-one class members. Matthews points to a kind of logo at the top of the plaque. The design includes a pelican, a bird not native to New England. "Why a pelican?" I ask. Matthews explains that the bird is part of the St. Paul's crest. "It's the symbol of sacrifice. The pelican plucks the meat off of her breast to feed her young," Matthews says.

After lunch I repair to the library where David Levesque, the library's technical services director, leads me to the school's archives in a locked section of the basement. He shows me two boxes of information on Hobey Baker, most of it photos but I am not much interested in pictures. I spend two hours going through the files and skimming two books on the history of the school. I find Malcolm Gordon's piece as well as copies of a few other stories. I stay in the archives about a half-hour beyond the point at which I'd planned to leave and, as often happens in such a case, I come across a copy of a six-page hand-written letter from Baker to former Princeton hockey teammate Wendel

Kuhn (Kuhn, a center, had scored Princeton's only goal in the 2–1 loss to Harvard). The letter is dated October 25, 1918, a few weeks before the end of the war and less than two months before Baker's death. I think the first page of the letter gives us a glimpse into Baker's character and the end of it dissuades me from thinking Baker's death was a suicide:

> *Dear Wen:*
>
> *Thanks for your letter. It was certainly interesting for of course I have not seen any of that part of the war and you really have no conception of what is going on on the ground when you are [flying] over the lines. Day before yesterday I missed the easiest chance I have had since I have been over the lines. I picked up a biplane . . . and got under his tail without his even knowing I was there. I think I wounded the observer but my machine had too damn much speed and I had to turn off to keep from running into him. It was just like missing a goal when you have gotten past the defense and have only the goal keeper to stop you. I guess I am pretty rotten.*

What surprises me most is the dispassionate tone of the first part of Baker's letter. Most of us define courage as advancing in the face of fear. It seems that Baker's type of courage was the much rarer absence of fear, an emotional detachment from what he was doing, which in this case was risking his own life while trying to take another's. I think I see how a man who equates an aerial dogfight with a hockey game could play hockey for years and take only one penalty. Hobey Baker was possessed by neither fear nor the anger that often masks it.

He was possessed by loyalty. Later in his letter to Kuhn, Baker, who had just taken over as squadron commander, writes of his plans to have the squadron's planes painted in Princeton's colors: "It may be rah rah and all that sort of thing but I am having all the radiators painted orange and black and am going to use a tiger head on the side [of the plane] for the squadron insignia, I think it will make a damn pretty machine."

It often seems that Baker himself is a machine. "Reading about Hobey is like reading about a saint," John Lorenz wrote in an email after our trip to St. Paul's. "Most saints are so perfect it's like they were cardboard and not real . . . like student council presidents who are also three-sport captains, they are above the fray."

But Hobey wasn't above the life-threatening fray of war and, at the end of his letter to Kuhn, Baker sounds introspective and almost vulnerable:

> Your letter was really damned good reading and as [my] father
> always says, my boy if you knew the pleasure your letters bring you
> would not begrudge the time and trouble to write them. The best of
> luck Wen and stay alive. . . . [I have spent four months] working over
> the lines and while I don't figure among the leading aces I comfort
> myself with that thought.

Here Baker sounds like a reluctant fighter, his tone far different and more human than the report of the man who, a few paragraphs earlier, was so cold in describing how he may have wounded the observer in a German plane. While Baker many times wrote of the excitement of war, incorrectly likening it to a sport (a sport is engaged in by cooperating opponents, a war isn't), he sounds here like a young man yearning for a war to end: "I wish you and I could get together so we could *leave* [emphasis Baker's] France together for I can see that you feel it the same way I do."

There is no cardboard in those words.

There was such gallantry, such great grace in the world. That was Hobey Baker's world, and it is good that it is not forgotten. For if it seems odd how his name keeps coming up after all these years, it is an oddness devoutly to be desired . . . it bespeaks our return, if only for a little while, to the time before we all of us fell from grace.
—George Frazier

After dipping my hand into Lower School Pond, I go back to my car and begin driving south on I-93, glad to have learned much *about* Hobey Baker but frustrated that he has been dead so long that it's now impossible to talk to anyone who knew him or skated with him. Because he didn't like talking to reporters and because sportswriting in Baker's day consisted mainly of game stories not features, there is no definitive Hobey Baker profile written during his lifetime. It is as though he is as elusive today as he was when he played; the essence of him dangles beyond our reach, and his seeming perfection is a stride beyond our understanding. How could hockey, the game that gave us the joking phrase "retaliate first," produce or even accommodate a player like Baker? It is tempting to say Baker helped produce hockey. But did he? Name a player like him? Where is his influence in the age of such moves as the facewash and the slew foot? Maybe Frazier was right and Hobey Baker was "a streak of chain lightning" no one ever saw before and we will never see again.

It is early evening when I arrive home and I take my manila folder of photocopied clips out to the back porch and begin flipping through them. The most interesting story is Ron Fimrite's in *SI*. The story ran on March 18, 1991, a time when Fimrite could do what we can't—talk to someone who knew Hobey Baker. Fimrite found C. Earl Moore, a retired investment officer then living in Rosemount, Pennsylvania. Moore was one of the four living members of the Princeton Class of 1914, Hobey Baker's class.

[Hobey] spent so much time playing and practicing that we never saw him much on campus, but, well, he was just the star of our class, of the whole school. His circle of friends was not my circle of friends but whenever I saw him, he always had a smile. . . . He was such an attractive man. He was so humble he'd never talk about anything he ever did in sports. . . . Oh, I don't think there was anyone at Princeton who didn't wish he knew Hobey better. He was so many things to us. But above all, yes, above all he was a gentleman.

Three years after Baker was buried in France, his mother, by now divorced and remarried, to Frederick Van Schutts, and with little money, arranged to have her son's remains disinterred, shipped to the United States and buried in the Van Schutts' family plot in West Laurel Hill Cemetery, Bala-Cynwyd, Pennsylvania. Moore tells Fimrite that the Van Schutts' plot is near his (Moore's) family plot and that Moore occasionally visits Hobey Baker's grave. Moore, beginning to weep, tells Fimrite: "I'll stand there and I'll know he's there under my feet, and I'll look down and I'll say, 'Oh, Hobey, why? Why, Hobey, why?' And there's no answer, you know. There never will be."

What moved Moore to tears was not only the memory of his fallen classmate. It was also his recollection of the anonymous poem on the headstone of Baker's grave:

> You seemed winged, even as a lad,
> With that swift look of those who know the sky,
> It was no blundering fate that stooped and bade
> You break your wings, and fall to earth and die.
> I think some day you may have flown too high,
> So that immortals saw you and were glad,
> Watching the beauty of your spirits flame,
> Until they loved and called you, and you came.

There is speculation that the poem was written by Baker's mother.

> It is odd, is it not, that the departed, no matter how dear, should inspire such invocation.
> —George Frazier

I've followed hockey for more than a half-century, followed it closely, at times earning my living in it, but it wasn't until the summer of 2007 that I learned much about Hobey Baker. For weeks the story, the thought of the man, wouldn't leave me. About a month after I'd visited St. Paul's School, I wrote to Bill Matthews asking if, when the black ice came, I could skate on Lower School Pond. I've skated in some historic and beautiful places, the old Montreal Forum, the Boston Arena, the Rideau Canal, the Boston Public Garden, Rockefeller Center, but of all hockey's icy surfaces, Lower School Pond is, to an American, the most important. I don't want to skate there for journalistic reasons or to add the pond's name to any sort of life list. I want to skate where Hobey skated not for the memory but for the honor.

I'll try not to look down at the puck.

GOODBYE TO THE BACKYARD RINK?

So we see some chapters of our lives
come to their natural end.
—Sarah Orne Jewett,
The Country of the Pointed Firs

My backyard rink makes my life better. It brings me closer to my children and grandchildren, keeps me active and has long helped to light my family's way through the long dark New England winter. But, as I write this, the rink is going on twenty-five years old and I'm in my mid-sixties. It's decision time: do I discontinue the rink of my own free choice? Or do I soldier on until the embarrassing and humiliating encroachments of age force a decision upon me? It's a tough call.

It was back in the winter of 1982/'83, and after several failed attempts, that I built a skating rink behind my home in Natick, Massachusetts. I did this by making a corral of plywood boards roughly 60 feet long and 35 feet wide, lined the corral with 6-mil. clear plastic sheeting and flooded the rink with a garden hose twenty-four hours ahead of an approaching cold front. Three days later my son Brian, daughter Tracey and two of their neighborhood friends skated on the backyard rink. That first ice wasn't strong enough to support adult skaters, this because I'd put in too much water and the ice never froze completely top to bottom. But the next winter I put in only as much water as was needed and the Bacon Street Omni was born.

The rink soon became a place for after-school hockey games, weekend skating parties and a family hockey tournament we called The Molson Cup because the names of the members of the two- or three-player teams that won the tournament were written in indelible ink on the side of an empty Molson beer keg. That keg still sits on my back porch ("it lives there," Barbara says). My name is not on it. I never won my own tournament. Never even came close. The now sun-faded names run from 1984 to 1997. The last year written on the cup is 1998 and, beside that, the cryptic note EL NINO, which refers not to a tournament winner but to a weather system that gave us such a warm winter that we never held the Molson Cup. Nor have we held it since. It was after *El Niño* that I first considered not building the rink. Brian, Tracey and their friends had gone off to college and, later, settled themselves into jobs and had long since moved out of our house. They occasionally returned for a skate or a scrimmage, but most of the time only Barbara and I used the rink. She enjoyed her after-work skates under the stars and I enjoyed solitary morning skates that amounted to little more than my cruising around snapping pucks into an empty net. On many of those mornings, I thought about what the rink had come to mean to me.

My rink connects me to the people I love. It was and remains an always-open avenue of conversations with my children, even during those early teen-age years when it was sometimes hard to find common conversational ground. So we found common ice instead. "How's the rink?" was the opening line of many conversations, some of which elevated themselves above hockey, most of which didn't. But they kept us talking to each other, playing together and, on the morning after a big snowfall, working together to shovel the ice. (And we did use shovels. It wasn't until 2003 that Barbara bought me a small snowblower.) The rink still keeps me in touch with old friends who occasionally come over to skate. And merely looking out the kitchen or den windows at the rink takes me back to my childhood, when most of my skating was outdoors on ponds and lakes.

It was late in the summer of 1999 that I first talked openly to Barb about not building a rink. "It's not just the kids being gone, it's that the boards get heavier," I said, the reference being to the four 4-by-8-foot ¾-inch plywood boards that formed what we call the "shooting" or "deep" end of the rink. I was in my late thirties when I first built the rink and, at the time, lifting those boards, each of which had three 10-foot studs attached to it, wasn't much of a problem. But, in my mid-fifties, I found the boards harder to lift. Barb suggested I leave the big boards in the ground year-round. I did and we had our rink for another four winters, or until the legs of the boards rotted and the big boards had to be pulled out and either replaced or repaired. It was now 2004 and I was sixty years old, a stage of life I described to two of my younger basketball-playing friends as "the time when you stop watching the shot clock and start watching the game clock."

"What do you think?" Barb asked me one summer night when we were having dinner on the back porch and looking out at where the big boards had once stood with their huge red block lettering reading THE BACON ST. OMNI.

"We'll see," I hedged. It was a careless mistake. You don't say "we'll see" to Barb because, as she explained to me early in our relationship, "'We'll see' is what my mother used to say when she meant no." Barb regards "we'll see" as wishy-washy and she regards wishy-washiness as the eighth deadly sin. Barb once had me stifling a laugh into my dinner napkin as she explained to a waiter that she wouldn't even consider ordering a rosé wine "because wine should make up its mind to be red or white. Rosé is just wishy-washy."

As the summer wore on, wishy-washiness gave way to certainty. "That's a wrap on the rink," I told Barb and anyone else who'd listen.

"Man, that's like pulling the trigger on Old Shep," said my friend Doc Kelly displaying his signature fondness for old pop music allusions and humorous overstatement.

I also got several versions of "Yeah. Right. That's what you said five years ago," these from Brian, Tracey and their friends.

But September gave way to October, the time of year when I had always begun digging post holes for the rink and recalling that great F. Scott Fitzgerald line, "Everything starts again when it turns crisp in the Fall."

But the rink wasn't starting again. Not this time. I was too old and the return was no longer worth the investment.

Mid-October came and went and the twin maples in the backyard laid down their annual carpet of red and gold leaves, a carpet I always left on the ground as a kind of natural cushion to protect the rink liner from sharp-edged stones, small sticks or anything that might have pierced it. But in the final lawn cutting of that year I set the lawn mower on mulch and ground the maple leaves into thatch.

I was surprised and relieved that Barb wasn't lobbying for the rink. I recently asked her why. "Because I didn't really believe you'd shut it down," she said.

But I think she did believe, at least for a moment. It was a day or two before Halloween and Barb and I were bundled up in sweaters and eating dinner on our back porch. It's a time-honored custom for us to dine on the porch as long as possible before falling temperatures and rising winds push us into the dining room like bears into a den. We were splitting a bottle of wine—as is also our time-honored custom—and were down to the dregs when Barb blinked first. "You're REALLY not going to put up the rink?" she said.

I took an exaggerated squinting stare into the yard. "You see a rink out there?" I said. "Anyway, it's too late to start now. I'd have to rebuild the big boards. It'd be like starting from scratch."

"You could get some people to help you?"

She was right. I could have. But I take the Emersonian view that the highest price you can pay for something is to ask for it. I had no intention of asking. Or blinking. The rink was dead.

Then Barb did what she does best. She ripped a shot into the only part of the argumentative net that I'd left open. "Demetre and Ella are going to be disappointed," she said, referring to our grandchildren. That was, as the pundits say, a goal scorer's goal. My most poignant moment on the rink had come about five years earlier when I'd skated a few laps cradling months-old Demetre in my arms. Whoever frames the question wins the argument and in that one sentence Barb shifted the case for the rink from a question of physical capacity, endurance, expense and time to one of legacy. Old Shep skated.

* * *

We went into scramble mode. Getting a late start on building an almost-new rink involved hustle and compromise. The next morning Barb and I went to Home Depot, where I hefted a ¾-inch sheet of plywood, the same kind I'd always used to make the rink boards. "Too heavy," I said. So I settled for ½-inch sheets. Instead of having three 10-foot studs on each board I had only two. Instead of digging 2-foot-deep post holes through our rocky soil I dug only 20-inch holes and hoped for the best. When the big boards were in place, Barb painted them white, no time for red lettering, while I installed the 2-by-8-foot boards that make up most of the circumference of the rink. We finished on the same day I almost always finish, the day before Thanksgiving. We needn't have rushed. The serious cold required to make ice (I look for teens or single digits) was late arriving. We didn't flood until after New Year's and didn't skate until January 20,

2005, when I took the season's first skate, later noting in our rink book: "First skate: Hey, Hey, Hey, it's Grandpa J. in seven degrees on a sunny day." On February 8, Tracey brought the grandchildren to the rink and noted in the rink book: "Bringing the next generation to the Bacon St. Omni."

Our grandson skated while his four-years-younger sister deigned to allow a succession of adults to pull her around on a red plastic sled from which she smiled and waved like Cleopatra on her barge. When Tracey passed a puck to me, I bounced it softly off Ella's sled and slid the resulting rebound to Demetre, who shot it into the empty net from point-blank range, falling to the ice on his follow-through. But the puck was in the cage and the goal had come through three generations. I can't remember many of the tens of thousands of goals that have been scored on our rink. But I'll never forget that one.

I'll also never forget what happened about twenty minutes later. It was one of those moments that will live in Bacon St. Omni lore and that makes the rink worth having. Ella, evermore Cleopatra-like, was now sitting in a steel-runnered chair that Tracey was pushing around the ice. I pivoted, crouched low and glided across the rink as if to put a soft hip check on Ella's chair. But in watching my granddaughter, probably so I'd be sure to miss her, I forgot how close I was to the low side boards. I unexpectedly skated into a low board, the top of which hit my leg about six inches above my ankle and sent me flipping out of the rink, head down and feet in the air. I landed on my left shoulder. Hard. Embarrassed, I bounced up and got back on the rink. "Grandpa Jack is funny," said a laughing Cleopatra, who probably thought the court jester had flipped himself out of the rink solely for her royal amusement. Tracey, who had a better grasp of the situation, momentarily turned into a play-by-play announcer. "And he's skating around trying to pretend that didn't really *really* hurt," she said. It hurt. But the hurt is long gone. The story will be around for as long as there is someone to tell it.

For the next two seasons I left the big boards in the ground and stored the smaller boards in the garage and the Bacon St. Omni continued through its twenty-fourth season. Then in the summer of 2007 I noticed two of the big boards were getting rickety. I'd painted most of the board legs with fence-post preservative when I'd put them into the ground two and a half years earlier. But, in our mad scramble to get the rink up after a late start, I'd forgotten to paint the legs of two boards. Those legs were now badly rotted. I decided to pull up all the big boards, replace the rotted studs and, later, reset each board more solidly. I was sixty-three now and pulling the boards out of the ground was a struggle. I first levered them a few inches out of the earth with a long-handled spade, then grabbed the bottom of the board and, in what was now an all-out effort, hoisted the board out of the ground and set it on the grass. I then carried the boards across the yard and leaned them against our big, steel-framed hockey goal. The last board sent me a message. I had the board clear of the ground and had taken a few steps with it when a gust of wind came up, pushing the board toward me and making it wobbly, heavier and harder to handle. I instinctively stuck out my right leg to use as a brace to help me steady the board against the wind. But as I put my foot down where the ground should have been, I caught the lip of our old vegetable garden and stumbled sideways with the sheet of plywood pushing me down. I somehow managed to jam my heel into the ground and found just enough strength to keep the board from pinning me like a wrestler. The wind subsided and I managed to prop the board up against all the others, angrily (and foolishly) shoving it into place as if personally affronted by its having almost fallen on me.

"Son of a bitch, I thought I was going to need Simon of Freaking Cyrene to carry that mother," I said, partly to the wind and partly to Barb, who was breakfasting on the porch. She said something about it being good to know that my Catholic school education hadn't been a complete waste and did I have a late score from the Yankees' West Coast game.

I said I didn't.

Barb has a theory about profanity in general and anger in particular. She says they mask other feelings, usually fear. I think she's right and, looking back on it, my momentary and partly synthetic anger covered up what I was truly feeling, fear of the limitations of age and of what those limitations ultimately portend.

It is early September as I write this and those boards are still leaning against the goal. Soon I'll replace the rotted legs with studs cannibalized from old rink boards. And in a few weeks I'll start digging the post holes in a way Barbara tactfully calls "age appropriate." That is, I'll dig one hole during halftime of a football game. Another during the break between games.

Others, one at a time, never working more than a half-hour, in the slanting light of late autumn afternoons when I like to be outdoors. I'll take it slow. And I'll probably finish on the day before Thanksgiving. The coming winter will be the silver anniversary of our rink, so there is no thought of discontinuing it this year. And I think the big boards, though somewhat dry-rotted where they touch the ground, are probably good for an additional year before they'll have to be replaced. But then I'll be sixty-five. The grandchildren will be more involved in their schools, sports and other activities and it is far more likely that we will be visiting them in Maine more often than they will be coming to see us in Massachusetts. And then it will be time again to figure out what to do with Old Shep.

In anticipation of that decision and out of genuine curiosity, I went to an online affinity group of backyard rink owners and asked the members what would make them stop building their rinks. I thought their decisions would have to do with kids growing up and leaving home. But the answers had far more to do with age and physical ability.

"I will only quit when I can't do the simplest of tasks and of course that [time] will someday come," wrote Pete Thalmann of nearby Hopkinton, Massachusetts. "But when that day comes maybe one of my boys will become the Ice Keeper and the next generation will inherit this great family tradition." Meanwhile, Thalmann, a sixty-one-year-old grandfather of six, has installed a refrigeration system under the concrete slab that is the base of his rink. He freely admits the system is a concession to age in that making good ice is now simply a matter of "throwing the chiller switch on one cold night in November . . . [and] refrigeration ain't cheatin'," he adds. "If you can justify it financially it's a godsend. Now you can have good ice from November to April. When you have a truly great family activity isn't more better?"

It is until your family scatters, you age and it all becomes a question of distance and time. But I get the feeling Pete Thalmann won't be shutting down his rink anytime soon.

Brian Phipps, a backyard rink owner from Grand Rapids, Michigan, takes an even stronger 'til death-do-us-part position: "I don't know that anything short of death or disability could cause me to give up our rink. . . . I sometimes think even just a week of skateable ice each year would justify the rink," he wrote in a letter. Then, apparently warming to the topic, Phipps added, "I'd build the rink for the one dazzling day when the sun shines bright in a cloudless sky and we skate all day in the arctic air, soaking in the light."

I think the Phipps' family rink will be around for a long while. But I don't think mine will be.

The legacy is secure. My grandchildren are old enough now to remember having skated on Grandpa Jack's rink. Others remember too. Three times Brian and Tracey's friends, people who as children and adolescents skated on our rink, have asked if it would be OK if they brought their own children to the rink. It is more than OK. It is what the rink is for.

But the question in a few years will be one not of legacy but of free choice. Do I want to give up the rink freely and of my own volition? Or do I want to hang on until I become rink building's equivalent of Willie Mays staggering around under fly balls? Of Sinatra forgetting the words?

Like all of us I prefer to make my own choices rather than to have those choices forced upon me.

The other side of the argument is that I also have a life goal of skating Ottawa's Rideau Canal when I'm eighty. Having my own rink is a great way to keep my legs in shape. But I could also do that at the town rink or at the pond down the street. The larger question is: what would fall and winter be like without the rink? In the preface to my book *Home Ice,* I quote Barbara who, vexed at one of Brian's young friends whining about the cold, said, "anyone can love summer, but to love winter you have to carry your sunshine around with you." That is the *raison d'être* for the Bacon Street Omni. And that is all that, so far, keeps me from pulling the trigger. What would it be like to look out my den window in winter and not see the rink? Perhaps even *one day* of skating with my grandchildren is worth the weeks of work. But then I think back to Valentine's Day of 2007, when we had what amounted to a slush storm; six to eight inches of heavy wet snow covered the walks and driveway when I arrived home in mid-afternoon after having been up since 4:15 in the morning. I was tired but I wanted to clear the driveway and walkways for Barbara's arrival a few hours later and before falling temperatures froze the slush. The wet snow kept clogging the snowblower and town plows kept pushing snow into the bottom of my driveway. I think I moved as much snow with a shovel as I did with the blower. I was exhausted. Then I looked at the rink covered with a deep layer of slush. I knew I was too tired to clear it. Worse, I knew what could happen if I didn't. And what could have happened did. The wet snow froze so that it was impossible to find a seam between skateable ice and frozen slush. The rink was done for the season. That was the first time, and so far the only time, that I didn't have the energy to do what I knew had to be done. But wasn't it also a harbinger of more such times to come?

We'll have our twenty-fifth anniversary year for the rink and maybe one more year thereafter. Then? I truly don't know.

We'll see.

ACKNOWLEDGMENTS

Writing is a solitary act but publishing a book involves the help of many people, foremost among them in this case is my editor Karen Milner at John Wiley & Sons Canada. After acquiring *Open Ice* on the basis of having read two sample chapters and an outline, Karen was relentlessly enthusiastic, patient and supportive throughout the writing, rewriting and editing of the book.

My thanks also to project manager Liz McCurdy, who endured and worked around my incompetence with all things technical. And my gratitude to copy editor Cheryl Cohen, who moved in and broke up the fight I was losing to the *Chicago Manual of Style*.

I could not have done the chapter on Hobey Baker without the help of my friend and St. Paul's School alumnus John Lorenz and St. Paul's Rector and former varsity hockey coach Bill Matthews who combined to get me access to the school's archives. St. Paul's School library technical services director David Levesque helped guide me through the archival material on Hobey Baker so that I could make best use of my time on campus.

I could not and would not have done the essay on the great goaltender Georges Vezina had it not been for the help of Dominic Simard of Chicoutimi, Quebec.

Friends and fellow goalies Gerry and his son Nick Hailer helped me with their insights about hockey in general and goaltending in particular.

Former US Marine photographer Jeff Sisto returned to my backyard rink, where he had skated as a child, to shoot the photo on the dust jacket.

My thanks also to my agent, Mollie Glick of the Jean V. Nagger Literary Agency who doesn't know a lot about hockey but is very good at arithmetic. And my gratitude also goes out to my friend and National Hockey League vice president of media relations Gary Meagher for helping me with access and information.

Grandchildren Demetre and Ella Fontaine make the game new for me when I see it through their young eyes. Thanks, guys.

And my biggest thanks goes to the former Barbara Spelman Baldwin of Northampton, Massachusetts, my skating companion, backyard rink party organizer, team enforcer, scrappy right wing and wife for forty years.

ABOUT THE AUTHOR

Jack Falla is the author of five books, most notably *Home Ice*, a collection of essays and memoirs that *The New York Times*' Robert Lipsyte called "literary hot chocolate that will warm your heart."

Jack covered the National Hockey League for *Sports Illustrated* in the 1980s. During that time he combined with *SI* photographer Heinz Kluetmeier to produce the book *Sports Illustrated Hockey*.

Jack and his wife, Barbara, live in Natick, Massachusetts, where, since 1983, they have built a skating rink—the Bacon Street Omni—in their backyard.

He teaches sports journalism at his alma mater, Boston University.